PLEASE
FEED
THE BEAR

How to Keep Your Boss From Coming to Your Desk Looking for a Snack

By

DR. KENNETH P. WOODCOCK

Disclaimer

Although this book contains references to US military services, specifically the United States Air Force, the thoughts, opinions, anecdotes, and lessons contained herein are the author's own. There is no official endorsement of this book or the material within by any element of the Department of Defense, the US Air Force, or any of the military units to which the author has been assigned. The use of the term *Air Force* is a simple reference and in no way is intended to imply official sanctioning by that military service. This book contains no classified information, and no references are made that would endanger military personnel or operations.

Copyright © 2013 Dr. Kenneth P. Woodcock
All rights reserved.
ISBN: 1483973956
EAN 13: 9781483973951

Library of Congress Control Number: 2013906487
CreateSpace Independent Publishing Platform
North Charleston, South Carolina

*For my wife, who believes in me no matter what,
My parents, who taught me the things in life truly worth knowing,
And for the Hellfish, who gave me the idea long ago and far away....*

The Menu

Hors d'Oeuvres
Introduction

Appetizer
A Taste of What's to Come

Entree
The Rules

Dessert
Something to Chew On

After-Dinner Mint
About the Author

Take Out Menu
For Quick Reference after the Meal

The Hors d'Oeuvres

Introduction

If you've made it this far into the book, you've got at least a little curiosity about something. Maybe it's leadership, maybe it's bears, maybe it's how feeding a bear is ever a good thing. Well, let me help you a little. This book is not about actual bears that live in the woods and look for handouts from visitors. This book is about how to feed the bear that you have unless you are independently wealthy or unemployed—and that bear is your boss. Sure, in this day and age we like to think bosses and employees are friends, but the boss is always the boss. After you or yours gets promoted, you can become good friends, even lifelong friends. I've been very fortunate to have that happen to me. But as long as you're the subordinate and they're the boss, you won't be true friends.

Bosses are like bears, and like the old saying says, some days you get the bear, some days the bear gets you. Bears have to eat. They like things to be quiet. They don't like anyone messing with their young. And you don't poke them. Make no mistake, there's a bear in your life whether you realize it or not. And this book is about how to feed the bear so you never have to say, "Well, it was one of those days where the bear got me."

This book has three main sections: Appetizer, Entree, and Dessert. The Appetizer should whet your appetite for learning the rules of how to take care of your boss so you don't become a snack. Your Entrée is twenty-nine rules for taking care of your bear. And Dessert is something to savor as you go back to work after consuming your meal.

The Appetizer

A Taste of What's to Come

Kinds of Bears

As you may surmise, there are different kinds of bears in the workplace just like there are different kinds of bears in nature. You have growly bears, grizzly bears, bears in captivity, Pooh bears, polar bears, you name it. You may have Yogi Bear for a boss. Or you may have Baloo from *The Jungle Book*. You may be unfortunate and have the bear from the movie *The Edge*.

This book is not going to help you figure out what kind of bear your boss is. Chances are you already know. Instead this book will help you figure out how to keep your bear from being hungry, because no one likes a hungry bear.

Bear Necessities

Bears have needs, which in this book are figuratively expressed as food—hence the name. What do bears eat? Pooh bears eat honey. You know, the touchy-feely stuff: chitchat about what you did over the weekend, your new clothes, or your new boyfriend. The sugary stuff that makes you feel like the two of you are buddies. But we know that bears don't really live on honey. So what is a necessity for bears? What meets the minimum requirements for their nutrition and keeps them from coming into your cubicle looking for a snack? The two R's: *respect* and *results*. If you feed your bear respect and results on a consistent basis, they'll be fed, full, and satisfied.

Now, here's the hard part for some folks. Say you don't respect your boss. Okay, that's something you'll have to adjust to and figure out how to handle. You may not have to respect them as a person to make them feel respected as a boss. Keep in mind you can pay respect to the position, not the person, and keep your integrity. But the boss needs to feel respected so he or she won't come looking for a snack.

The results? You have to produce. You have to give the boss something useable and useful. Depending on what kind of work you do, those results will be different. This book won't help you create results, but it will help you package and present them to your boss as tasty snacks that keep your bear from being hungry.

Bear Survival Rules (the Entree)

Just like rules for dealing with bears in the woods, there are rules for surviving with bears in the workplace. Of course the rules are different; after all if you went supine and stayed absolutely still every time your boss came into the room, that probably wouldn't bode well for your career. Or if you made a lot of noise and angrily charged your boss when he was at the end of the hallway, that wouldn't be good either.

There are 29 of these survival rules. Some are longer than others. Some are more complex. But each rule in some way helps you feed your boss either respect or results. How did these rules come about? Fair question. I first codified and put them out to some of my folks in 2007. I was and still am a proud member of our nation's armed forces, so these rules, like a lot of things, had their genesis in our military. We were in Iraq, and we were responsible for hundreds of people scattered all across the country. Our job as the headquarters was to keep up with what all those folks were doing and ensure they were organized, trained, equipped, and operating like they should be.

Now, the folks assigned to me were not headquarters-trained desk jockeys. They expected to come to Iraq and be involved in the mission outside the wire—helping the Iraqis rebuild their country, running convoys, etc. None of them had anticipated preparing PowerPoint slides, giving briefings, writing memos, or any of the things headquarters folks do. So I had to help them. They needed some guidance to succeed. So I wrote these rules based on what I expected from them. I told them basically what it takes to feed me as a bear.

Yep, I've been a boss. And I'm a bear to work for, and sometimes to work with. I developed my rules and my style based on the folks I worked for and with over the years. Now, some of you will already be saying that since a lot of my background is military, the rules don't translate. You can't expect people in normal jobs to react and act like those in the armed forces. Well, I disagree. The common denominator in all organization is that they are made up of people. And people are still people. Think about where you work. Is there a uniform? Sure there is. Suits, ties, dress shoes. You all kind of look alike, with some small differences. That's how military uniforms look too, with small but distinct differences between them.

And yes, if you tell someone to do something in the military, they're going to do it. Pretty much all the time. How is that different from where you work? If the boss says, "Get me some coffee," don't you get it? There are disagreements and discussions in the military all the time, just like where you work. And there are meetings and briefings and conferences, and office politics everywhere. Because people are involved. And people are always people.

So, if a set of survival rules were developed, put out, and used during a combat tour and they worked, why wouldn't they be useful where you work? I think you'll find they will be. After all I put them out to my folks whenever I get a new organization, and at first there's resistance, much like you may have as you read along, but eventually they realize that if they feed me what I ask for, I don't come growling down the halls looking for a snack. And how many bears do you think have small snacks?

So here is your Entree:

1. Never, never do or allow anything illegal, unethical, immoral, or stupid.

2. Know your boss's priorities. Work those as if they were your own because if you don't prioritize like your boss, your boss will reprioritize for you. Know your boss's boss's priorities too, and how what you're doing fits. If you don't know the priorities, ask.

3. Don't hesitate to ask your boss what to do if you're uncertain about anything.

4. Don't ever sign your boss's name to anything.

5. Avoid "The Boss Wants" syndrome.

6. Never keep anyone waiting on the phone. Call back.

7. If you say you're going to get back to someone, ensure you do, and do it in a timely manner.

8. Be available to anyone who wants to see you. Never treat people like you're busy or too important to listen to what they have to say.

9. If it's an emergency, you'll know. If it isn't, take time to analyze and think before you act, speak, or write. Get someone to read over your e-mail, paper, or staff package before you hit "send."

10. No surprises. Bad news doesn't get better with time.

11. If there is a problem brewing, your boss will want to know about it early, so give them a heads-up as soon as possible. Bosses don't like being blindsided.

12. There's no such thing as too much relevant information on an issue. Stick to the facts and leave your ego and emotion at home.

13. Punctuality is the courtesy of kings. Be punctual; don't waste anyone's time, especially your boss's or your own.

14. Meetings should be uninterrupted and an interactive exchange. Ask a lot of questions. Discussion and debate are part of the development process. Once the boss decides, though, debate ends and you move out.

15. If you don't ask, your boss can't say "yes."

16. No one knows your job better than you do. After all, you're the one doing it. So no one is in a better position to make suggestions for improvements than you are. If you have an idea for how to make something better and you don't voice it, you can't blame anyone but yourself if things don't change for the better. See rules 10 and 15.

17. Take the time to do it right because there is not always time to do it over. And doing it over usually requires an explanation of why it wasn't done right in the first place.

18. Be your boss's best source of information on what's happening.

19. If you've briefed your boss's boss on something, ensure you brief your boss on it too.

20. If someone higher in the organization talks to you and makes an inquiry or an observation, ensure your boss knows. People in high places and their staffs don't make casual statements.

21. Paperwork is not the enemy, but it may be your means to defeating the enemy.

22. If a suspense lapses and you haven't completed the task, and your boss doesn't ask for the work, don't assume it's been forgotten. The boss won't forget it's due. Neither should you.

23. Extensions and waivers can be granted for almost anything, but not if you don't ask. (See rules 15 and 17).

24. Keep track of who you've talked to and when.

25. Writing things down develops and enforces discipline of thought. If you can't put it on paper, keep thinking.

26. Bosses speak with a purpose. If they make a suggestion, it's an order. Using "please" and "could you" is really just them being polite. Make no mistake: they're not talking to hear themselves talk.

27. When you speak, do so with precision.

28. When you write, do it right.

29. Lastly, only you know if you gave one hundred percent to everything you did that day. The boss can gauge and get close, but only you will truly know if you gave it all you had. Your one hundred percent is all that can be expected. It's also all that should be accepted. If you think doing the minimum is good enough, let your boss know. You can be sure they'll help you find somewhere else to spend your time, because you're wasting theirs.

Bon appétit...

Entrée

The Rules

RULE ONE:

Never, never do or allow anything illegal, unethical, immoral, or stupid.

Okay, so this one sounds pretty simple, right? Don't do, or if you're a supervisor, let your people do, anything illegal, unethical, immoral, or stupid. But in life the simple things are sometimes the hardest. Your boss will have zero tolerance when it comes to this rule. If you do something illegal, you're done. Your boss can't help you or else he goes to jail too. If you do something unethical, your boss can't help you because then he gets disbarred, fired, or disciplined too. If you do something immoral, depending on where you work you may get fired and your boss might too. Doing something stupid sounds harsh. Who does something stupid on purpose? No one, right? How many times have you and your buddies at work cooked up a little recreation, and right before you kick it off you look at them and say, "Watch this"? Yep, you might not have considered whatever happened next stupid, but your boss probably did.

So why are these such a big deal? Well, believe it or not your boss probably does value your contributions to the organization. If he didn't, he'd fire you and find someone else to do it. And doing anything illegal, immoral, unethical, or stupid puts your boss in a bad spot. No matter what they have to take action, and usually it's unpleasant. Most bosses who remain bosses don't like to discipline people. They'd rather reward them for a job well done.

But doing something illegal means you have to get disciplined at best, jailed at worst. And you bring the organization along with you. Stupid things detract from productivity, from getting the job done, and could get someone hurt—all things bosses prefer not to have happen on their watch. Unethical things bring up lots of questions bosses don't want to answer, like: "What kind of section are you running anyway?" "Why did your employee think that was an okay thing to say?" "Don't you know the company's policy on this kind of behavior? Haven't you communicated it to your employees?"

All in all, doing things that are illegal, unethical, immoral, or stupid causes you problems and causes your boss problems. And when the boss has problems, the boss looks for snacks. You made the bear hungry.

Respect
How does obeying this rule show your bear respect? First, your boss plays by these rules (or should), so he expects you to as well. The rules (be they legal, ethical, moral, or common sense) are what hold the organization together as norms or mores. Violating them shows disrespect for the organization and what it stands for. Your boss, as someone who probably believes in the organization to a significant degree, is probably personally insulted if you break the rules. It isn't a matter of "well, my boss didn't do it, so it's not really a reflection on him." It does reflect. And a lot of times it reflects personally, and that means it's a matter of respect. By obeying the rules, you show respect. You feed the bear what it needs.

Results

Obeying this rule helps generate results? You bet it does. Think how distracting it would be for your boss if you were in some legal trouble at work because of something you did. How much time would your boss spend on investigating, reporting, answering questions, implementing new policies, training the other employees, and then recovering from the incident? And that's if your boss keeps his job.

Now imagine how much time it would take to recover your standing in the company after an unethical or immoral act. How much credibility would you lose? And therefore how much would you not be able to contribute because people didn't trust you anymore? You would be of less worth as a contributor to the team, so you would bring fewer results. This is taking away something the bear needs. However, if you contribute and play by the rules, you don't create these other priorities. And believe me, they would be priorities for your boss. Getting whatever you did off *his* boss's radar would be a huge priority for your boss. By not creating this additional time thief, you enable yourself, your boss, and your fellow workers to concentrate on the work that needs to be done. You can get results. You can feed the bear.

RULE TWO:

Know your boss's priorities. Work those as if they were your own because if you don't prioritize like your boss, your boss will reprioritize for you. Know your boss's boss's priorities and how what you're doing fits. If you don't know the priorities, ask.

You must learn what your boss finds important. What does your bear think is the first order of business every day? The overnight sales report from the overseas market? The quality of the end-of-day summary reports? The upcoming day's event calendar? What the latest news story about the company is? What the latest new story about the company's competitor is? If you don't know what your boss thinks is the important thing to be doing, you may inadvertently find yourself doing something the boss thinks is unimportant. And that may be a chance for your bear to have the first snack of the day in the form of reprioritizing your day for you.

If you can take care of the things your boss cares about first and foremost, your boss will move along and look for something else to do. For example let's say you're in charge of the overnight reports from overseas, and your boss likes to have them early in the day so she can prioritize work for her other divisions based on what happened overnight. So you come in and you think checking the scores from the late games on the West Coast is the first thing you should do because not much happened overnight and the reports aren't that exciting. You don't forward them right away because you figure your boss can see them on the server as easily as you can. Thus she doesn't have them when she opens up her e-mail account first thing in the morning.

Do you think she's going to shrug her shoulders and go on to something else without knowing what happened overnight? Probably not. In fact she'll probably pay you a visit first thing, and it won't be to find out if your team won the big game last night. You might as well coat yourself in honey and present yourself to her when she walks into your cubicle because you've just made yourself breakfast. Her breakfast.
An extreme example? Maybe. Maybe not. I've seen it happen. Think about your boss: Do you know what she thinks is important for you to do first thing in the morning? What overriding principles or priorities does she have for you or your section? If you don't know these things, you may find yourself not doing them through no fault of your own other than you didn't ask.

Bosses don't mind explaining things if you ask them. After all, if you're asking for help, why wouldn't she give it to you? Everyone likes to be the one who gets asked, the one who is seen as knowing the answer. If you ask your boss what her priorities are, she'll light up, and he'll probably kick back in her chair and begin to give you her version of how things are. Listen closely because in those moments you'll learn a lot about your boss and her priorities. Take notes if you want to or if you can. Then go back and figure out how what you do each day helps contribute to the priorities your boss explained to you, and make those priorities your own.

If you really want to help, always keep your boss's priorities in mind when pitching a new idea or a solution to an existing challenge. And if you know your boss's boss's priorities, even better. You may be able to make your boss look good to her boss, and that will pay big dividends for you. So there's another good question to ask your boss: what are her boss's priorities? See what kind of answer you get.

Respect

Taking care of your boss's priorities is an easy way to feed your bear respect. If you are doing what your boss thinks is important, you give your boss the impression you think it's important as well (even if you don't think it is). People tend to think that people who agree with them are good; in fact some people actually evaluate others based on how much or how often they agree with them. Does this tendency create yes-men? Perhaps, but that's your boss's problem if she doesn't value discourse and discussion. For you, the main thing is to feed your boss respect by knowing, understanding, and working on their priorities. Later we'll discuss how you can influence what those priorities are, but for now you need to know them and work on them. After all, you want to have your boss's job eventually, or your boss's boss's job, so you'll have to do what she wants so she can move up. Then you can move up and make your own priorities. Feed her respect by respecting what she thinks is important—and doing it.

Results

Your boss will measure results against their priorities. If your boss's priority is for you to analyze the sales figures for the last two years, and instead you analyze the production figures, you will have done good work and probably done it correctly, and it's probably something that eventually needed doing. But it's not what your boss wanted done first, so it really isn't a result that counts for her. And your boss counts, so you need to do things that count for your boss. Figure out what those things are and do them first; then you can do the things you think are important, and they will be much easier because you won't be getting e-mails and phone calls, and "come see me" notes to explain why priorities one, two, and three aren't complete. Feed the bear results she wants to see based on her priorities and you'll avoid being a snack.

RULE THREE:

Don't hesitate to ask your boss what to do if you're uncertain about anything.

A lot of people have trouble with this rule. They think that asking their boss a question will create the impression that they don't know what they're doing. They may even feel like talking to their boss is a bad idea. Some people have the notion that the less interaction you have with your boss, the better. Nothing could be further from the truth. The more you interact with your boss, the better. The more you know how your boss thinks, what your boss wants, and how to get it for him, the better it is for you. Avoiding your boss only keeps you from learning things you need to know. Does this mean you need to be a sycophant and hang on your boss's every word? Not at all. It does mean you need to have open, regular interaction with your boss.

People who believe it's better to get forgiveness than permission hate this rule because it means you're actually asking your boss what he want done before you do it. People who want to do their own thing don't like being told by the boss what the boss wants, so they don't like this rule. But isn't it easier to find out what your boss wants done, then do it rather than guess and hope you make the right decision, and then if you guess wrong do it all over again? This rule doesn't imply that the boss controls every situation or action. It means when you aren't sure or you don't know, that's when you ask for clarification and guidance, which you know your boss will probably enjoy giving you.

Now, if you take this rule to an extreme and you cease to be able to make any decisions for yourself and are constantly asking the boss what to do, you may have a problem. But if something new or unexpected arises and you're not sure what to do, just ask.

Respect

How does this rule feed your bear respect? It directly gives the boss respect for his opinions, his guidance, and his way of doing things. It values how the boss wants something done. It shows deference to the fact that if there is a preferred way, it's the boss's way. And it enables the boss to be a mentor, a teacher, an imparter of wisdom because you're asking him, he's not telling you. The boss doesn't have to come down and direct. It's a teaching moment for him, a chance to pass on what he's learned over the years in a way that is collegial and encourages further interactions. It feeds the bear a nice, tasty morsel of respect, and it costs you nothing.

Results

The results in this case are pretty apparent. You ask the boss what he wants done, then you do it. Your boss gets to tell you what he thinks needs to happen and then you go make it a reality. This enables the boss to outline what he wants and, often, how he wants it, and then you know exactly what to do to make it work. It eliminates guessing on your part, which means you have more time to concentrate on getting results, and that means more results for your boss. It eliminates ambiguity from what needs to happen and enables everyone involved to work toward the desired result without having to guess what it should be. It's another easy snack for your boss, and it keeps the bear's hunger pangs away from your cubicle.

RULE FOUR:

Don't ever sign your boss's name to anything.
This one dovetails with rule one about illegal actions. Pretty much anywhere, in any organization, you can't sign someone else's name to a document. Now, some people try. They figure they have the boss's signature block, and they see enough of the boss's signature that they can do it. Most justify doing it to save the boss time or because the boss "doesn't need to bother with this," or even thinking the boss would want them to just go ahead and do it. But the fact is a person's signature is a precious commodity, and there are numerous reasons why you don't want to sign your boss's name to anything.

First, if your boss doesn't actually sign it, she probably doesn't know what it is. Which may be what you want, but that will likely come back to haunt you. Especially if someone who is above your boss in the food chain sees or hears about it. How do you think that'll go? The executive vice president of the firm asks your boss about a requisition for new office furniture for your section, and it's the first your boss hears of it. Where do you think your boss will go once she gets out of her meeting with the VP? Yep, straight for your cubicle. Get out the honey.

Second, if your boss doesn't sign it, she doesn't have a chance to support it if it's a good idea. So you may lose the opportunity to get your boss behind a good idea. If she doesn't see it, she can't expand the scope, give more resources, or even advocate for more high-level endorsements for the idea or program. You're cutting your boss out of the loop and shortchanging her of the chance to support you.

Third, you're putting your boss in a legal bind, depending on what you've signed her name to without her knowledge. And if it comes out that you've signed it, there could be legal consequences for you as well. Forgery, conspiracy, or other criminal charges may come your way. See rule one for why you don't want to do anything illegal.

Respect
This rule feeds your boss lots of respect. It respects her authority to sign documents you can't. It respects her integrity by upholding the fact that if it has her name on it, she signed it. It helps you show respect for your boss by giving her the chance to put his name on good ideas and prevent less-stellar ones, and keeps her in the loop on what's going on in the organization. It shows respect for the rules of the organization and reinforces that rule one applies to you and your section.

Results
This rule gives you the chance to get real results for your boss by keeping her in the loop. It allows your boss to endorse things through the power of her signature, enabling you to really get things done every time she signs her name to a requisition, a memo, or an idea. It reinforces your ability to operate freely within the bounds of your own authority to do things because you're staying in your lane. It keeps you working on real work and not having to run around making sure your boss doesn't have to answer embarrassing questions about memos she never signed. It frees you to operate without having to look over your shoulder for your boss to come snacking, enabling results to flow.

RULE FIVE:

Avoid "The Boss Wants" syndrome.

You know how this goes. You're rushed. Time is short. People aren't getting done what you need so you can finish a project. So you do what you've done since you were a child. You get backup from the highest authority figure you can: mom or dad. Or, in this case, your boss. But he doesn't know about it. How did it work out when you got your sister to clean the garage because you told her Mom said she had to do it, and then Mom found out? Not too good for you, right? Same thing here. If your boss didn't say, "I want this done right now, today, by the end of business," you may be in for some discussion with him when he finds out you used his name/authority/power for something you wanted done. Especially if it wasn't something he thought was a priority.

Violating this rule creates problems for you on multiple levels. First, you lose integrity with your coworkers and subordinates. If they find out—and they will—that you used the boss's name in vain to get them to do something, they'll start to wonder what else you've been dishonest about along the way. And once they lose that trust in you, you'll find it very lonely and very difficult around the office. Second, you're demonstrating to your boss that you can't get things done on your own. Maybe your persuasive powers aren't what he thought. Maybe your leadership ability is lacking. Maybe your management skills aren't up to the job you have. You've planted seeds of doubt in your boss's mind about whether you're right for the job you have, much less a promotion. Third, it's similar to signing your boss's name to a document in that you're tarnishing his reputation without his knowledge.

Now, if the boss really does want something done, that makes it easy. That one you won't have to sell because the boss will make it clear it's a priority. In a memo, a meeting, a conference call, or an e-mail, there will be tangible proof that what the boss wants is X, Y, or X. Then you don't have to reinforce it or tell it to anyone because it will be apparent to all. And that's how it should be.

Respect
How does this feed your boss respect? It demonstrates that you respect his authority to decide what he wants; you're not presuming to know. It shows respect because you're not putting words in the boss's mouth. You're letting him get his message out in his own way.

Results
How does this rule contribute to results? It keeps integrity among the leaders in the organization. It makes it clear that if you say the boss wants it, then the boss wants it. It preserves your integrity, which enables you to be a better leader and employee, and it preserves the boss's integrity by not having people running around declaring things in his name that aren't true. It also prevents people from checking up on everything you or your coworkers say the boss wants because there is a lack of trust. Saying, "The boss wants…" only when it really applies keeps the boss from having to answer questions over and over about what he wants, freeing him up to concentrate on what he's doing and freeing you up to do what the boss wants done. Because if the boss sees things getting done, the boss won't get those hunger pangs.

RULE SIX:

Never keep anyone waiting on the phone. Call back.

This one seems like it's a tad weird in the middle of all these rules about how to take care of your boss. After all if the boss calls, you don't put them on hold, do you? You answer right away, yes?

But think about this: If not your boss, who do you put on hold? Customers? Clients? Other employees who are inferior in rank to you? Peers? Why is it okay to put them on hold but not your boss? Is their time less valuable? Are they less critical to the operation of the organization? Just because you can put them on hold, does that mean you should?

Of course putting someone on hold to get someone else to pick up the phone is perfectly acceptable. That's not the kind of waiting we're discussing. This is about putting someone on hold while you look up a piece of information or ask someone else a question. It's about reinforcing your authority to put that person on hold, in effect saying, "Your time is not as important as mine, so you can wait while I do this other thing, then I'll get to what you want." Whether you intend to or not, that is the message you're sending.

Why would your boss not like that? Because people don't like to feel unimportant. Because customer service and good operating practices contribute to better-running organizations. Because small things like putting people on hold can snowball into disputes over who sits in what chair during a meeting or who gets what parking space, and pretty soon your boss is refereeing status-symbol disputes between employees instead of managing and leading the organization to achieve its goals.

So instead of putting them on hold, take down their question or find out what they're calling about and then tell them you'll call back with the answer. It shows that you know what they want is important and their time is important as well, and you won't waste their time while you look up an answer they need. Besides, it frees you up to get a good, solid, factual answer rather than rush and get one that may be less than completely accurate. After all when they're on hold, how much time do you really take to get them an answer? Telling them you'll call back gives them the chance to do something else while they wait; it gives you the chance to get them a good answer (preventing your having to answer it again anytime soon); and it sends the message that you value their time and you won't waste it by keeping them on hold.

Respect
Does this feed your boss respect? It does. It shows you respect the fact that your boss wants her employees to be professional and above petty squabbles, and to send the right messages to customers, clients, and fellow workers. It demonstrates that you understand the value of time—not just yours but everyone's inside and outside the organization, and that you understand how to help manage that precious resource. It feeds your boss respect because it shows you genuinely respect others, and that means the respect you pay your boss is genuine as well.

Results
Does this really generate results? You bet it does. How many times have you answered the phone, gotten a question, put the person on hold, looked up what you thought he wanted, answered him, and hung up, and then ten minutes later he called back for further information or clarification? Think how much time you would have saved if you had asked him to tell you what he wanted, told him you'd call him back

with it, and then gone and found the answer, taking your time to get a complete one? It would have prevented the second callback, freeing you and him to continue to work on other things. And if it was a client, you prevented him from being exasperated, irritated even, by respecting his time and then providing him with a complete, well-researched answer to his question. It feeds people lots of things when you don't keep them waiting on the phone: respect, time, energy, and all that contributes to results, which is what your boss can snack on instead of on you, which is what you want.

RULE SEVEN:

If you say you're going to get back to someone, ensure you do, and do it in a timely manner.

This one goes hand in hand with rule six. Seems like something you would do anyway, right? Ever had anyone say they'll get back to you on something and then they never do? Ever had to call back two or three times to get an answer even after you were told, "I'll get back to you"? How did that make you feel? How willing were you to ask that individual for help or information after that? How frustrated were you with that person and, by extension, their section, division, or organization?

What about if you call someone, say a peer of yours in another section, and ask for clarification on a presentation you saw her make? She says she'll call you back, but instead one of her subordinates calls you with the information. How would you feel? Do you think you'll be real pleased with your peer? Or will you feel like she just put you in your place by having her subordinate call you instead?

This rule is about creating the positive perception that you value the people you come in contact with and that you take the time to find out what they want to know, and then you personally get back to them with it. Is that important? You bet. Does your boss really care? Of course. How other people perceive you and your organization is critical to him.

If other divisions or sections see you and your shop as closed off, high-minded, or conceited (think that way about anyone or any other section you work with?), it makes it harder for him to fight for you with his boss, which bosses do, just not always when and where you can see it. And it makes you and your co-workers less likely to compete favorably for those subjective things everyone wants like promotions, bonuses, trips, perks, and so on. But if everyone thinks your section is a bunch of prigs, you won't be heading to the conference in Miami; you'll be staying in the office.

Respect

Does this really feed your boss respect? Not directly. But it feeds respect to other people, those around your boss, and that means they in turn feed your boss respect. It's like a food-chain effect: you respect the people in your boss's peer's section, they don't talk bad about you to their boss, and when the bosses get together, no one talks to your boss about those rude, stuck-up employees of his, and he feels the love. And you avoid being a snack.

Results

Does this help bring you results? Of course it does. If people know you're going to get back to them when you say you will, they'll rely on you more. And the more they rely on you, the more you can get things done. The more positive perceptions you create among sections and organizations outside your own, the more likely those people will be to help when you need it, co-operate when it's required, or do you a favor when you ask for it. And those things help you create results. And results feed the bear so you don't have to.

RULE EIGHT:

Be available to anyone who wants to see you. Never treat people like you're busy or too important to listen to what they have to say.

This one falls in line with rules six and seven. It's about perceptions—positive perceptions. Unless you have absolutely no interaction with other human beings (in which case you don't need this book), how you act will create perceptions among your coworkers, peers, subordinates, and superiors. And positive perceptions make it easier for you to get done what you need to do, which is what your boss wants. Treating someone like they are the most important person in the room at that time goes a long, long way and can't truly be measured in terms of value.

For example when I was a brand-new young officer, I was in an organization of about six hundred folks, all of whom were combat-trained, and we were on alert in a pretty austere location. Now, in this organization there was a Chief Master Sergeant. He had been in the service longer than I had been alive. In fact he had already been in grade school before I was even born, so he had been around and he knew what was what. His job in the organization was to keep his eyes and ears open to everything that was happening and to advise the commander on basically whatever he thought the commander should know. Now, this meant the Chief had to keep an eye on morale, on discipline, on supplies, on training, on equipment, on operations, on personnel, on everything. In an organization that ran twenty-four hours a day, seven days a week, with no holidays and no weekends. Needless to say, the Chief was busy.

So there I was, fresh off the boat, so to speak. And I didn't really know what I didn't know, much less anything else. But when I happened to walk into the Chief's office one day—I still think it was an accident, but I can't be sure the Chief didn't somehow orchestrate it—there was the Chief, looking at his computer with a stack of paperwork in his inbox and a regulation manual open on his desk. He looked up and saw it was me, and what did he do? I fully expected him to usher me out, politely of course, or to keep doing what he was doing. But he didn't. He closed the manual, turned off the computer monitor, got up, came around his desk, offered me a chair, sat down, and talked to me for almost an hour about what the troops expected out of their officers, things I could immediately do to create the right atmosphere (perception again), and things like that. He didn't have to do that. I certainly didn't expect him to do it. And I know he had much more important things to do that day than spend that time talking to me. But he did it. Because he took the time to make me feel like I was the most important person he would speak with all day, even though I intellectually knew I wasn't, I felt that way. And feelings go a long, long way toward creating the right perceptions.

How do you make people feel when they come in your office? Do you treat everyone like it will be the most important social interaction of the day for you? You never know when one of them will be. And what will they say when they leave your office? "Wow, she really listened to me and was genuinely interested in what I had to say," or "She didn't hear a word I said. She spent the whole time looking at her e-mail and watching to see what phone calls were coming through the switchboard. That's the last time I bring up any of my ideas to her"? Which perception do you want to create? Which one will foster more creativity, more energy, more enthusiasm among your employees?

Make no mistake, your boss watches your employees and how they act. That and how they perform are the true measures of how you are performing. If they're working hard and getting things done, the boss credits you for it. If they're moping around in a fog, wandering aimlessly just watching the clock, the boss blames you for it. Your employees get you promoted, your boss brings you the news. If you're taking care of them, they take care of you.

Respect
Does this feed respect to your boss? Again, in a food-chain way it does. It creates a feeling of mutual respect around the office, and that flows upward to the boss. It makes the boss perceive that you respect their values and the things they think because you're creating an environment where people value each other's time, and that means no one is wasting any—something every boss detests. So yes, there is a respect snack in there because you're keeping your boss from having to spend time sorting out employee complaints. And that means less chance of you becoming a snack.

Results
Does this help you bring your boss results? Absolutely. By creating perceptions of extreme value among your employees, clients, and peers, you foster an atmosphere where people want to get things done, know how to do them, and ask for help if they need it. All those things help you achieve the goals and priorities your boss has in mind, which translates to results—a tasty snack for any boss.

RULE NINE:

If it's an emergency, you'll know. If it isn't, take time to analyze and think before you act, speak, or write. Get someone to read over your e-mail, paper, or staff package before you hit "send."

I usually work in an organization that responds to real emergencies. We have lights, sirens, and so on to get us where we need to be in a hurry. In that kind of situation, you really don't need to be asking questions about what to do and when. Those matters should have been addressed in prior training or exercises. When it happens for real, there's not much time to be teaching. And you'll know when it's the real thing. It will be abundantly clear, and if you've done what you should in terms of training, your reaction will come as second nature and you'll be fine.

But emergencies, thankfully, don't happen too often. In fact they're rare, which means you have time to think about what you're going to say, send, or do. A few minutes of preparation before you fire off an e-mail may save you lots of explaining on the other end, depending on what you send. Taking the time to think it over gives you a chance to step back and consider the implications and ramifications of what you're sending before it is forever on the e-mail server. Consider who is going to read it, who they may pass it on to, and what your audiences will think of it. How many times have you hit "forward" on an e-mail just because it was easier than rewriting what someone sent you? You can bet your boss will do that too. So keep in mind that anything you put in an e-mail, a memo, or a staff study will become public. It will. So think about that before you hit "send."

And then there is the "get someone to read it over" part of this rule. Folks often come to me and say, "I don't have time to let someone read everything I write." That may be true. But if it's an important e-mail, or a memo you're trying to get signed, a second pair of eyes could save you a lot of trouble. We are all blind to our own writing styles, and in some cases we don't even notice the errors or typographical missteps we commit. And words matter. The choice of word can be the difference between success and failure of a memo or an e-mail. If you don't know your boss's hot-button words, you need to find out what they are. And your boss has them, believe me. Some supervisors don't like to be called "boss" while others don't mind or don't care. I've seen e-mails actually addressed to "Boss" before and it was okay. But other supervisors would see that word and immediately forget the rest of the e-mail because all they would think is, *He knows I don't like to be called that and he started the e-mail off with it. I wonder what else he isn't doing that I ask him to do.*

Your choice of words is critical in your communications not just with your boss but with everyone. So getting someone you trust to look over your communications is critical. It will help you make them better, and that second person may see something you missed. It also enables you to ask the important questions: "What am I asking for in this email?" "What do you think my most important point in this memo is?" "How does it read?" "Did I use any of the danger words?" "What impression does this message create?" "Is it clear what option I think is the best one?"

If you have someone review your work with these questions in mind, you will produce better products and your message won't be garbled in transmission, and you won't spend hours explaining why you said "x" when you should have said "y" while what you really wanted to get across was "z."

Respect

Does this rule feed your boss respect? Of course it does, and in a very specific and effective way. It shows that you value your boss's time enough to make sure any communication with her is clear, concise, and well constructed. It shows you respect her by not assuming she has time to sort through your jumble of sentences to find the right one. One of the things I usually do is put a one-sentence summary of the e-mail in the beginning. It's called the BLUF (bottom line up front). My going-in position is that my boss may read only that one line, so I get all the important stuff into it.

My second technique is to keep the body of the e-mail to six lines or less. If I can't get across what I need to in those six lines, I keep working on it, or I realize it's a complex issue that may be better handled with a memorandum, a staff package, or an in-person conversation. Also keep in mind that memorandums are just that: memorandums. They should be one page if you can. If you can't keep it to one page, maybe the issue needs something larger, like a staff study or a set of briefing papers. A memorandum should be on point, concise, and brief. If you're using it to explain an issue, you've missed the point of what a memorandum is supposed to do for you. The memorandum exists to put out to the organization an authority figure's perspective on a single issue. Not preparing memorandums that way is a misuse of the tool, and that is disrespectful to the rules and norms of the organization. And your boss likes it when you add value to the organization, not devalue it by using things in an inappropriate manner.

Respect flows when you're only sending things of value to your boss. You're not wasting time and electrons on frivolous e-mails just to show her you're working, or sending memorandums that are really policy papers or research studies you want to get approved. You're respecting your boss's time by not wasting it, leaving her ample time to do the work she needs to do, which won't include snacking on you for sending her an e-mail she needed to give to her assistant to decipher.

Results
Does following this rule help you generate results? Yes. In fact it exponentially increases your ability. The less time you have to spend on explaining your original e-mail with follow-up e-mails, the more time you have to do your actual work. I've met a lot of people who think their jobs are to watch their e-mail and answer it. E-mail is a tool to get the real work done, whatever that happens to be, but there is a growing segment of the workforce that seems to believe that e-mail is actually work. It's not. It's just electrons that, when used properly, can contribute to getting work done, but it's not actually work itself. So by using it efficiently, communicating effectively, and sending, preparing, or transmitting only analyzed, well-thought-out communications, you increase your ability to do your real job, which is what will keep your boss from coming to snack on you and your huge, server-clogging e-mails.

RULE TEN:

No surprises. Bad news doesn't get better with time.

Surprises are okay and appropriate in some settings—birthdays, anniversary parties, spontaneous getaways with your significant other, etc. But at work no one really likes surprises, because in that venue they're typically not good. The idea of work is for things to go well. So when there is success, it shouldn't be a surprise. If you're working and the expectation is for it not to go well, you need to find another job. The expectation should be for good things to happen, so when they don't it should be a surprise. And that means surprises are bad. And no one likes bad news or bad things to happen, least of all your boss.

So what should you do when there is bad news? Be honest. It won't get better with time. In fact the chances of it becoming worse with time increase with every passing moment you don't tell your boss about it. Because at some point, the question may come up—"When did you know this?"—and if you knew about it and didn't tell your boss, the next questions may be, "What else is she covering up?" "Why didn't she tell me?" "Is there more going wrong than just this?" And those are not questions you want your boss to ask.

Now, does this mean that as soon as anything bad happens, you should immediately rush to your boss's office with cries of "the sky is falling!"?

No. But it does mean that if you see trouble brewing, you give your boss a heads-up. Letting him know a project is falling behind as soon as it falls behind means that when the deadline comes and it's not done, your boss won't be surprised. He may not be happy, but he won't be surprised. Surprised and unhappy is not a good thing. It makes the bear hungry.

So be honest when things aren't going well. Some people call this *expectation management*, but that's more of a spin than what you really need to do. You don't ever want to spin your boss. Be honest about what's going on and let your boss know why. If the project is behind because the expected resources weren't delivered due to weather problems, let him know. If the new software isn't indexing the files properly and so your audit is behind, tell him so he can get the software gurus to help you. Don't keep pressing on with a project that isn't working without letting your boss know it's not working. Sometimes the answer may be, "Keep at it and we'll see what happens." And in that case, do so. But don't think that you'll get points with your boss by persevering for perseverance's sake. The boss wants results, and letting him know how it's progressing enables you to give him results. Granted, if the project is a mess, it may not be the results he wants, but if you're not hiding that it's going poorly, it won't be the results that surprise him.

Does this mean you should whine to your boss about every little thing that goes wrong in your section? Not at all. What it means is that you need to know what your boss expects (see rule two) and ensure that if what the boss thinks is happening isn't happening, you've let him know. Your boss doesn't need to know every little hiccup you encounter on the way to completing that month's tasks, but if a task isn't going to be completed, the end of the month isn't the time to notify him, especially if you knew since the tenth that you weren't going to make it. If you're operating that way, you might as well get out the honey.

Respect

Does this rule feed respect to your boss in good doses? It does. It lets your boss know you have a handle on things to the point where you can tell him what's happening and what struggles you're encountering. It feeds respect because you're letting your boss know where he can help you. Something going wrong at your level means your boss has a chance to help at his level. The fact that you're giving the boss the opportunity to help you is a sign of respect: you respect his knowledge and experience and know that by coming to him, he'll share both with you. And that keeps the hunger pangs at bay.

Results

This rule enables you to continue to produce results even when things aren't going so well. The results will just be different from what you (or your boss) previously expected. But they will be results nonetheless, and that's the important part. And by letting your boss know, you may get additional resources you hadn't anticipated, which may enable you to get results on a scale you previously had not be able to, and that's a good thing. Open, honest communication with your boss about what's happening gives him a chance to help when possible, intervene when needed, and adjust expectations when warranted. And that creates results—a tasty treat for any bear.

RULE ELEVEN:

If there is a problem brewing, your boss will want to know about it early, so give a heads-up as soon as possible. Bosses don't like being blindsided.

If this rule sounds familiar, it should. It's a lot like rule ten when it comes to no surprises. But there's a difference in shading here. Sometimes there are problems brewing that shouldn't take you by surprise. Sometimes your boss will ask you to do things everyone knows will be problematic. The trick here is that you need to keep your boss in the loop, especially if the problem has something to do with an area or a project that affects other parts of the organization or your clients. She needs to know about anything that goes outside your area or her area sooner rather than later. This gives her the chance to intervene if necessary and to do her upward communications (remember, she's got a bear of her own to feed) if required.

For example in one place where I worked we had a new, electronic gate system installed. To get in you showed your little card to the card reader, and the gate was supposed to open automatically and close behind you. Sounds good, right? And it was. Except when they designed it, they didn't take into account that in the wintertime, it snows. And ices. And often does both at the same time. And that made the card readers not want to function and the gates not want to move. Ice clogged the tracks of the gates. So what could we do? Just let the gates freeze and then tell the boss? Or disable the system and then tell the boss?

Well, as soon as it started to snow and ice, I briefed my boss on the potential problem and suggested we implement a plan to monitor people coming and going (which is what the cards did for us). This enabled us to keep the same level of security while not having the gates frozen shut or open and people not able to get in or out of areas where they needed to be. Now, I could have just let the gates freeze shut and then we would have disabled entire areas of the installation. Or I could have just opened them all and let people run back and forth without any kind of monitoring. Either one of those outcomes would have been within my purview. But I choose to give my boss the heads-up early so he could weigh in, and he could brief his boss so that when someone else said something to my boss's boss, it was already covered. It made us look proactive (which we were) and enabled us to control the message (which we did) by not hiding the problem or making it less important than it was.

So if things are going but not necessarily like you hoped, let your boss know. Believe it or not, your boss has a huge interest in helping you when and where she can. Your boss looks good when you look good, so give her a chance to help when you need it. It doesn't make you a weaker leader by letting your boss know things are getting rough. In fact it makes you a stronger one because you have the integrity to tell it like it is.

Respect
Again this rule feeds your boss a snack of respect because you trust her to do the right thing in a tough situation. You're showing her you rely on her judgment and experience to help you when you or your shop is struggling. It's also a reminder that she, as the boss, has influence, power, and control over situations in your shop and he can demonstrate her authority in a way that helps you and your folks, and that's a good thing for her. Bosses like to snack on good things when they can.

Results

This rule helps you get results, and that means your boss gets results. Letting your boss in on what's up lets her help with what comes out at the end. That ensures she gets the results she expects and can adjust if need be. Open, direct communication about the situation enables you to be results-oriented instead of playing "I've got a secret" or "I hope no one finds out," and that means more time to get things done because you're not spending any time covering up what didn't get done. Covering things up or hoping things aren't discovered is the equivalent of feeding your boss empty calories. You always pay for them later.

RULE TWELVE:

There's no such thing as too much relevant information on an issue. Stick to the facts and leave your ego and emotion at home.

A lot of people struggle with this one because so much of so many people's identities is mixed up with what they do. They believe that what they do defines who they are, so they take it personally whenever something isn't done the way they believe it should be done. You know these people. I'm sure you've met them. They think that the way they put the agenda together is the only way that works, and they become irate if it isn't done their way. They insist everyone always addresses them by their title.

But here's the secret: who you are is so much more than what you do. If your identity and sense of self, especially your self-worth, are tied to your job, you are in for a rough time because eventually you will change jobs. Sooner or later you'll stop doing what you're doing now, and you'll do something else. And if the way you see yourself is tied to the job you have, you're going to have a tough time. It really is just business. It's not personal. If you take everything that happens at work personally, you will be miserable because a lot of not-nice things happen at work. Now, some things you should take personally: Pride in what you do. Your integrity. Your dedication. These are things that belong to you. But they are also more than just how you are at work.

Those are innate characteristics you have outside of work as well, and huge advantages to bring to work.

So what is this rule really about? It's a reinforcement of the fact that making decisions is not personal. They're made based on what's best for the organization. Now, if you can balance it so the needs of the most people are met along with the needs of the organization, that's great. But ultimately the organization's needs will come first or the organization will cease to be.

That's why it's good to have as much information as possible on an issue. The more your boss knows about the implications of a decision or a new program, the better informed she will be. And the better informed your boss is, the better her decisions will be. The trick is to provide information that is factual and free from bias. Most everyone can tell when you have a position on an issue versus an interest. A position is something you take; it is rigid and inflexible, as if it were set in stone. An interest, on the other hand, is a principle or an objective you want to see met, though how it's met is really not important to you. For example a position would be that you want dinner at six o'clock on Friday night at a particular restaurant. An interest would be that you need to have dinner on Friday night, and you would like it between five and eight o'clock. If you go into the restaurant you want with the position and all the reservations are taken, you will likely be frustrated because you won't meet your positional goal. But if you have the interest in mind, an opening at that restaurant at seven thirty would mean you get to eat there that night, which is really what you wanted.

Positions are tied to emotions and notions, and that makes them more difficult to defend and advocate for, and bosses see that. When you advocate strongly and passionately for something without much information to back it up, it gets harder to sell the higher you go. But if you can back it up, you can present your interests in a way that makes them seem more attractive and more logical, and that makes it easier for your boss to approve or advocate for them as they go up the line.

I see a lot of folks who really don't like it when a decision goes against what they recommended. I ask them why they're so upset, and usually it comes down to, "They didn't do what I wanted." So their position wasn't met. Then we talk about what was decided. Was it legal? Was it ethical? Did it meet all the regulatory guidance? Did it make sense from a larger perspective? Almost always it does. Because those are things bosses look at when they make decisions.

Now, it's natural in a large conglomerate for one part of the organization to prefer it done one way and other parts of the organization to prefer it done other ways. Not every decision will turn out the way your shop wants. Usually the arguments that win are based on facts and information, not on emotion or conjecture. So you need to give your boss information and facts and leave the emotion out of it.

For example when my boss needed to select an officer to come work directly for him, he asked all the subordinate unit commanders to come in and talk about the candidates. I had three candidates, and I really couldn't afford to lose any of them. There were five or six other commanders in the meeting, and each came in saying, "I can't give up anyone, and here's why...." Their reasons?

"Officer M is new and is just learning the job."

"Officer K has been in her current job for only six weeks and needs to stay there for a while to learn it."

"Officer A just got back from deployment and is settling into the job."

Are these valid reasons? Sure. But they're not as heavy on facts as they could be. Of course the boss didn't want to have to take anyone, but he needed someone for the greater good of the bigger unit. And arguing that someone was new or needed development was more an emotional than a factual argument.

When it came to me, I took a different approach. "Sir, if you need them, I can give up officers X, Y, and Z. Officer X is currently deployed and won't be back for three months, so he won't be available next week, but when he returns you can have him. Officer y leaves for deployment in two weeks, so he's effectively gone for the next eight months, so I think he is probably not a good choice. And officer Y leaves next month, so you can have her for five weeks if you wish and then she'll be gone as well. That's all I have available, but if you need them you can have them."

So did I lose an officer? Nope. Now, part of it was that mine were being sent overseas, but part of it was that my arguments were based on facts. And facts feed the bear.

Respect
Does your boss understand that emotions play a part? Of course she does. Does your boss know you're passionate about your work? Sure she does. And you can demonstrate it by showing how much information and facts you gather on an issue. When you present ironclad, well-researched information on an issue, you're paying your boss the respect of not playing on her emotions. You're respecting her enough to let her see the facts and decide for herself. You're not telling her, "You should do this because it's right." You're respecting that she can see what's right for herself.

Results
How does this help you feed your boss results? If you have your facts straight and you can make an argument logically and dispassionately, you are generating results. You're equipping your boss with facts, and facts go a long way in a hotly contested meeting among bosses. If all you're feeding your boss is emotion and conjecture, those snacks will run out of steam fast. Facts remain facts no matter what, and those facts, they are what get you, and ultimately your boss, results.

RULE THIRTEEN:

Punctuality is the courtesy of kings. Be punctual; don't waste anyone's time, especially your boss's or your own.

Kings don't really answer to each other. They rule their kingdoms as they see fit. But to be courteous, kings are punctual when meeting one another. Why? Because even they can't control time. It waits for no one, not even royalty. So, to be courteous to each other, kings respect the value of being on time and do not try to assert dominance or control over one another by being late. They appear when and where they say they will because they can, and because they know it's the right thing to do.

This one seems like it's pretty easy to follow, right? But how many times have you walked into a meeting late? How many times have you said, "I'm only a couple of minutes behind—it won't have started yet"? If your organization has meetings that don't start on time, what does that say about other things going on in your place of work? Time is a resource that cannot be replaced in any way, but it can be easily squandered, lost, misused, or abused. How do you think your boss regards waste? I bet you already know. So why would you waste time, a most valuable resource, by being late?

In my organizations the meeting starts on time whether I'm there or not. If I'm detained somewhere else and can't be there on time, that doesn't mean the meeting waits. Whoever is the next senior person begins the meeting, and I get there when I can. Meetings should be for the people attending, not the boss. Believe me, your boss is rarely surprised by something said in a meeting.

Having said that, I once had a boss who had a rule I still use: if the meeting starts and you're not in it, you can come in and sit down, but you don't get to talk. Most meetings in the military have a tradition at the end where everyone gets a chance to speak if they need to. But if you didn't come in on time, you lose that chance. Harsh? Maybe. Effective? Certainly.

Now, will you be late sometimes? Sure. It happens. But if you know you're going to be tardy, let you boss know ahead of time. Don't be late just to be late. Some people actually advocate being late as a way of asserting control over a situation. If everyone is waiting for you, you have more power than the person who is nominally in control of the meeting—unless you run into someone like me, who knows that little trick and doesn't put up with it. Just plan to be on time. One of my former commanders put it like this: If you're ten minutes ahead of time, you're early. If you're five minutes ahead of time, you're on time. And if you're on time, you're late. Plan to and be on time. It gives huge nonverbal reassurance to everyone when they see you can get to a meeting on time. If you're perpetually late, it causes doubts. People start to wonder what else you are not doing the way it should be done.

Respect

This is a huge morsel of respect for your boss. I'm sure you've seen the look in a supervisor's eyes when someone comes late to a meeting. It disrespects everyone in attendance. Of course if you know you'll be late and you tell your boss ahead of time, you're not late—you're excused. Being on time and understanding the importance of same demonstrates to your boss that you value his time more than your own. It shows you respect the resources of the organization and are a good steward of those resources even the intangible ones like time. Being on time means you've got things organized, understand what's important (in this case your boss's time), and can prioritize accordingly. If you can be on time to the meetings or ready for the conference calls, no one is going to be looking for you, wondering where you are. No seeds will be planted that will later germinate into thoughts of *I wonder what he's up to when I haven't asked him to be in the meeting.* Feed your boss this tasty morsel of respect and you'll end up with more time on your hands to do your job and less time in your boss's office explaining why you were late.

Results

If you can get to work on time, get to meetings on time, and not waste time, your ability to get results will improve. You won't have to document where you are all the time for your boss. You won't have to answer questions about your tardiness. You won't have to come up with reasons to casually run into your boss to explain how the traffic was bad on the way to work and that's why you weren't there to take the first-thing-in-the-morning call. Yes, bosses know that trick too.

If you're on time, it reinforces your competence. It subtly enhances your integrity. It demonstrates that yes, you do know what you're doing and you do have your act together. It makes you a less appealing snack because you are where you're supposed to be when you're supposed to be there, and that means you're getting the job done, enabling your boss to snack on results instead of your excuses.

RULE FOURTEEN:

Meetings should be uninterrupted and an interactive exchange. Ask a lot of questions. Discussion and debate are part of the development process. Once the boss decides, though, debate ends and you move out.

So you've managed to make it to the meeting on time. But you forgot to turn your phone to "vibrate." And it rings while your boss is making a particularly important point. How do you feel now? Or, better yet, how do you feel when you're in a meeting and someone actually answers his or her phone at the table? What message does that send?

The message is that even though you're in the meeting, other things and other people are more important. Is that what you want to tell your boss? It's what you say every time you text during a meeting. It's what you say when your Blackberry rings and you answer it. If you're going to be in the meeting, be there. If it's a real emergency, someone will come down the hall and come in to let everyone know. But if you want to contribute to the discussion, it has to be your focus.

Questions during meetings are not bad things. Now, you can ask bad questions, and people sometimes do. But questions that are thoughtful, piercing, and, most importantly, on point are always useful. Not all bosses run their meetings so people can ask questions, but most do. Most subordinates, however, don't like to ask questions in meetings.

They hope either the meeting is almost over or they don't want to look foolish, or they think their questions will embarrass someone. If you're fortunate enough to have a boss who entertains questions and debate, don't hesitate. Bosses want to know what you think about a topic. Most of the time that's why they hire you: for your mind, your experience, your perspective. If you don't give that to them in the form of questions and input, they may question whether or not you're right for the job.

Do you always have to ask questions? No. Do you always have to have input? No. But when you have a good question, one that relates and won't embarrass anyone at the table, ask it. Chances are you're not the only person who has that question.

The last part of this rule is sometimes called the "don't disagree with the boss in public" clause. Once the boss decides on a course of action, you need to support it. Even if you don't agree with it, as long as it's legal and ethical and no one is going to get hurt, you have to support it. Especially in public. Especially to the rest of the staff. Your boss hired you in part because you can carry the message to the other members of the organization and sell it to them as if it is your own idea even if it isn't. Will you agree with every decision your boss makes? Probably not. Will your boss take your perspective into account? Hopefully. But once you've given your input and the boss decides, that's it. No walking around saying, "Okay, here's what the boss decided to do. It's not what I wanted, but she said we're going to...." That undermines your boss and eventually will undermine you one way or the other. Either your shop will see you as weak and unable to fight for them effectively or your boss will hear you're not carrying the message properly for her. Either way you'll be looking for work.

Respect
This rule feeds respect much like rule thirteen. It values the time spent in a meeting. It shows your boss you are focused and committed to the task at hand and that other things can wait. By keeping your phone silent and not taking calls, you demonstrate that you understand your boss has important things to say and you have important contributions to make to the discussion. Asking questions demonstrates your interest and buy-in

to the organization and feeds your boss respect because it shows you are interested in the same things she is. Discussing and being involved also shows that you value the outcome of the meeting, which, since your boss called it, must be important to her, and that shows respect. Finally, by carrying the flag and carrying out the boss's direction without griping or undermining it, you show respect for the boss's authority and position. It also shows loyalty to the boss by ensuring gripes go up the chain of command, not down—a huge morsel of respect for your boss to chew on.

Results
Being involved in the discussion will help you get your concerns and the concerns of your subordinates heard, which can directly translate into more resources, modified policies, or even new projects. That means more results, and results are tasty. But if you aren't involved, if you don't ask questions, if you don't contribute, you may lose out on the chance to improve the situation. And that could mean fewer results. Being fully engaged in a meeting means you're looking for ways to do things better, you're advocating for your shop's interests, and you're involved in the decision-making process. And those things will enable you to feed your boss results, which taste much better than feeding your boss your Blackberry after it rings during the staff meeting.

RULE FIFTEEN:

If you don't ask, your boss can't say "yes."

A lot of people don't like to be around senior members of the organization. Some think that in a gathering with the bigwigs, the best you can do is break even. But your boss—even though a lot of people don't believe this—wants you involved. He wants to know what you think. He wants to hear your ideas. He wants to help you succeed because when you succeed, he succeeds. After all if he doesn't have someone trained to replace him, his boss won't promote him either.

So you have to ask your boss for things from time to time. He isn't all-knowing, so he may not know that you need something to make the current project exceed expectations. Unless you ask for the additional resources, he will never know and you'll settle for a mediocre performance instead of a stellar one. If you don't ask, you're denying your boss the chance to say "yes" and approve a great idea or endorse a particular action. And you want your boss to say "yes."

Saying "yes" enables your boss to contribute, to be part of the action, and to be involved in what you and your shop are doing. It gives him a chance to help you, and it enables your boss to give you something you've asked for. It makes it so your boss doesn't have to direct all the time; instead he can be responsive to your needs.

Now, does this mean that every time you ask for something you should expect your boss to give it to you? No. But it means that every time you don't ask, you definitely won't get it.

Respect

This rule feeds a host of respect to your boss. It reinforces that he is, in fact, the boss. It enables him to grant requests—something he doesn't have to do, but in this case he gets to do. And that is a huge morsel of respect. It also means you're respectful of your boss's role and you're not out just doing things and planning on getting forgiveness. You're acknowledging that your boss has the authority and enabling him to use it wisely by saying "yes" to you. This is a great rule to remember because it's easy to forget. The simple act of asking your boss for things will open communication lines, create dialogue, and make it so your boss is not only more aware of what you're doing but also more inclined to support it by saying "yes." And that's much better than your boss saying, "Hmm…I'm hungry."

Results

Will you get better results when you ask your boss? You bet. You may not think so at first, but over time, when you realize he will support you when you need it and knows you'll come to him when he can help, you'll start to get more resources, be able to take more risks, be trusted with more responsibility, and get more results. The difference between good and great outcomes could be a simple matter of asking, "Can I get two more people detailed to this project?" If your boss says "yes" and you get them, he gets better results. If you don't ask, you don't get the "yes" and you don't get the extra help, and you get so-so results, which don't sit well in the stomach of a bear. So ask for help, give your boss a chance to say "yes," and see what you can get done.

RULE SIXTEEN:

No one knows your job better than you do. After all you're the one doing it. So no one is in a better position to make suggestions for improvements than you are. If you have an idea for how to make something better and you don't voice it, you can't blame anyone but yourself if things don't change for the better. See rules ten and fifteen.

This one relates to rule fifteen because if you have a great idea and you don't bring it to your boss, she can't approve it or endorse it. Similarly, if you see a problem in your shop and you don't bring it to your boss, that may create a surprise, and bosses don't like surprises (rule ten).

So what does this rule really want you to do? It's asking you to think about not just what you're doing but how you're doing it. Is there a better way? Can you and your shop do what you do more efficiently? More effectively? Is there something that will make it so you work smarter, not harder? What would make things run more smoothly? Are there opportunities you're missing?

This rule imparts trust to you—trust that you're not just going through the motions day after day and that you're looking for opportunities to do things better. It acknowledges your stewardship of the organization's resources and expects you to find ways to keep things moving forward and improving.

So what do you do if you see a chance to make things better? You do research. You figure out what it will cost, if anything, to implement your idea. You gather the data. And then you present it. You craft a proposal, make an appointment, and go see your boss. You present your analysis and your research, and you ask your boss for her perspective. And then you wait and see what happens. Will she implement your idea? Maybe. Will she modify it? Probably. But will it make things better for you, and more importantly your folks? If you did your research properly it will.

I had a chance like this once. We were in an organizational structure where we had people assigned to either a "staff" or an "operational" function. The two sections were completely separate, so we essentially had everyone reporting to two different bosses with no real way to prioritize which one took precedence. What to do? Well, one boss would be better than two, so I took time and crafted a proposal that merged the staff functions and the operational constructs—I took the staff and made their work operational in orientation. I thought it out and wrote it up and then I took it to my boss. Now, did it work like I first envisioned? Not at all. Instead of just fixing our little location, all our locations nationwide adopted it…all because I did the research and asked the question.

Of course you may be thinking that sure, with years of experience and education I should be able to come up with good ideas. But I drew up this proposal when I was twenty years old, not even out of college. A good idea is a good idea no matter where it comes from, so take the time to think about what great ideas you have and then figure out how to make them reality. Your boss will be excited and say "yes" if you do your homework.

Respect
Like some of the other rules, this one feeds your boss respect because it reinforces that you care about making the organization better—something your boss is interested in as well. It demonstrates you aren't just punching the clock to draw a paycheck but

are interested in making things better, and that resonates with your boss. It shows respect because you come to your boss with not only an opportunity but also a way to take advantage of it. It shows that you respect the boss's authority to make decisions and implement new ways of doing things. It's a tasty snack, and one you'll be glad you prepared.

Results

Will this rule help you get better results? If you do your homework and suggest good ideas it will. You'll probably be amazed by what you can find that can be improved just by looking around your office. Most of the time that's really what it takes: time to look around. Sit and think about what happens throughout the day in your shop, and see what you can make quicker or more streamlined, or even eliminate. When you find ways to do things better, you'll have more time to get things done, and that means results. And results always taste good to a hungry bear.

RULE SEVENTEEN:

Take time to do it right because there is not always time to do it over. And doing it over usually requires an explanation of why it wasn't done right in the first place.

This sounds like something your parents told you when you were in school, right? Well, it's still a good rule to follow. The main reason you can and should take time to do it right the first time is this: you usually have the time. Your boss gives you the time to do things that need to be done, and unless it's an emergency (see rule nine) you will have time to work on it. So don't squander the time you've been given by doing a sloppy job. Take the time and do it right. Will it mean taking more time? Perhaps. But if you don't do it right the first time, what will happen? You'll get to do it over again—if you're lucky. Of course, depending on what it is, you may be looking for work if you don't get it done right the first time.

If you have to explain why something wasn't done right in the first place, usually it's not a particularly pleasant discussion. Bosses aren't big fans of their folks not doing things right when given the chance and the resources. So if you don't do it right the first time, not only will you get to do it over, but you'll probably get some "help" doing it right the second time, and that won't be fun. , Not to mention the fact that in all likelihood you'll have to do it over on your own time, not the boss's, so save yourself time and do it right the first time.

Now, sometimes I hear people say, "It's good enough," or, "If the minimum wasn't good enough, it wouldn't be the minimum." Okay, if that's what you want to believe, enjoy your life of mediocrity. Would you choose the doctor who got C's in medical school over the one who got A's? Probably not. So why would your boss choose the person who barely gets it done on time and barely meets the minimums over someone who does it right the first time? C is a passing grade, and meeting the minimum keeps you from getting fired (maybe). But is it what your boss is looking for out of you?

Respect
Taking the time to do things right the first time shows you respect the resources (time, money, personnel, equipment, etc.) your boss has entrusted you with to get the job done. Doing the job right shows your boss you respect the stewardship she has granted you over your piece of the organization's mission. Ensuring you take the time to do it right shows you understand the value of your and your boss's time and you won't be wasting it by doing only enough to get by. You spend the majority of your time each day at work, as does your boss. What message do you send her when you don't give her your best effort every time? If you're not respecting your boss enough to do the best you can the first time every time, what kind of dish are you preparing to feed your bear?

Results
Results are what this rule is about, for the most part. It's about taking time to produce the best results the first time every time. Do-overs are expensive—they waste time, resources, energy, and patience. No matter what kind of bear you have, I guarantee there is a limit to her patience, and do-overs wear on patience in a huge way. Doing things right the first time feeds your bear good, solid, filling calories while a sloppy, lazy job is empty calories that only leave the bear hungry for something else.

RULE EIGHTEEN:

Be your boss's best source of information on what's happening.

Have you ever wondered how your boss seems to know a lot about what's happening around the organization? Keep in mind your boss wasn't always a boss. Chances are she started out as something else in the organization. In fact, once upon a time she may have had your job. And she probably was good at it and got promoted. Which means she knows how to do your job as well as you do, and she knows where you get your information because that's where she used to get it from as well. And now she has even more resources and more ways to find things out because she can poke her nose in where ever she wants—after all she's the boss.

If you really want to know what's happening in an organization, there are always people who will be more than happy to talk to you. If you have a cafeteria in your building, the people who work there know what's going on—I guarantee it. Why? Who watches what they say when they're ordering a salad? Who really pays attention when the busboys are cleaning up the table next to them? Most people don't notice these folks much at all, so they talk about whatever they want and don't think twice about who may be listening. Believe me, the folks in the cafeteria know who's eating lunch with whom, what they're talking about, and what the latest gossip is. And if you befriend them, they'll tell you.

The Rules

Now, am I saying you should spy on your fellow workers? Not at all. I'm telling you that your boss knows how to get information about what's going on from various sources, some of which you may not even think about or notice. The security guards who monitor the comings and goings in the buildings and grounds know more about who's doing what when and where than anyone else. There are a host of ways your boss can and probably does get information.

So what to do? Simple. If there's something the boss needs to know (see rules ten, eleven, and twelve), make sure she hears about it from you first. Covering it up or trying to keep the boss from finding out something will only make it worse. Discussing things openly and honestly with your boss creates the trust that is essential for you to be able to do your job, and it means your boss doesn't have to take time to go around and ask other people about things you should have told her.

One time, about a month before I arrived to take command of a base, an individual was detained and escorted off because he had been belligerent during an air show. There were witness statements and all kinds of documentation that showed he had violated the rules and done things that caused him to be escorted off the installation. But he was very upset and thought he had been wronged—so much that he threatened to call all kinds of people and make a big fuss about how he had been treated, etc., etc.
When it came up later in one of my staff meetings, my folks told me about it and I filed it away for reference. As it turned out, this individual did indeed make phone calls and try to make a big stink about the whole thing. In fact he called some of the senior officers on the base to complain to them. Of course I didn't know this until the disgruntled individual left a voicemail for one of my folks as well. My people, much to their credit, immediately came and told me.

So what was there to do? Well, I got a copy of the voicemail and all the reports, and I beat feet to my boss's office. Unfortunately, one of the people who had been called was faster, so my boss had already heard about it. But one of the most critical questions he asked me was, "When did you learn he had called so and so?" When I told him

I had learned of it only moments before I'd come to see him, he was satisfied. It appeared not all those who worked for my boss always came forward in such an expeditious manner. So even though what I had to say wasn't pleasant, and even though someone else had beaten me to the initial notification, my version of what took place became the one my boss took to his boss because I had not tried to cover it up, and had come to him with it as soon as I had learned of it.

Respect

This rule feeds huge respect nuggets to your boss. It means you trust her with anything and everything in your part of the organization. It promotes open and direct communication with your boss and shows that you want her to be involved with and knowledgeable about what goes on down in the trenches where you work. It makes your boss feel like one of the team even though, as the boss, she won't play much in the game. She's still on the squad and should get to know what happens in the locker room at halftime.

Results

This rule helps you feed results to your boss in a few ways. First, if your boss's main diet is information, your bringing the data is a good thing. It shows your boss you can produce what she wants and are willing to bring it to her rather than make her come looking for it. Second, if your boss is talking to other people about what's going on in your shop, you have to check if the people she's talking to have the real scoop. If they're feeding your boss bad data, she may ask you about it and then you'll be in explaining mode instead of delivering mode, and it's always best to be the one who delivers your news yourself.

Third, if your boss is checking up on what's up, you're less likely to enjoy her trust, and that makes it hard to work. It makes every request more scrutinized, every statement more analyzed, and generally you have to ensure everything is crafted to prevent anyone from looking at it for hidden meanings, etc. So it means you spend more time explaining and justifying than you do actually working, and less time working means less results. That makes for a hungry bear.

RULE NINETEEN:

If you've briefed your boss's boss on something, ensure you've briefed your boss too.

Okay, this rule gives people who don't like math a headache. Basically it boils down to this: Your boss doesn't want to be blindsided by his boss, especially if what blindsides him is something you told his boss. So make sure you tell your boss anything you say to his boss.

Do you know your boss's boss? Can you recognize him? If he's at a reception and comes over to you, will you know this is the person who signs your boss's checks? If you don't already, you need to. Because the higher up people are, the less likely they feel like introducing themselves. They're going to assume you know. And they're going to be inquisitive. The higher up in an organization senior leaders are, the less in the know they feel about what's happening in the workplace. And for the most part, they're usually right. Most employees shy away from encounters with management, so anytime a big boss has a chance to talk to the line employees, he takes it. And he asks questions. Is this a bad thing? Not at all. Can it be a bad thing? It can be if he asks you a question, you answer it, and then he tells your boss what you said before you can tell your boss about it. (See rule eleven about not being blindsided).

So what can you do? Do you avoid contact with senior management? Not remotely. In fact senior management is where you want to end up one day, so you need to learn to behave like them. The best way is to be around them when you can. Does that mean you'll have to talk with them? Of course. Just keep in mind that anything they say, they're saying for a reason (more on that later) and they'll remember it. Don't ever be fooled into thinking senior members of the organization aren't sharp as razors. They remember names, faces, places, and, for the most part, everything anyone says to them. Those skills are part of what it takes to be senior management. Should you be afraid of them? No. Should you be a little nervous? Perhaps, but that's normal.

The main thing to remember when talking with anyone, but especially senior management, is to be honest. Say the senior vice president of the firm asks your opinion on something. If you have one, give it. If it's contrary to what your boss has said, be cautious. Explain that your opinion is based on what you know and is only your opinion, and that for the real perspective your boss is the better person to speak with. But if pressed, be honest. And then find your boss and let him know what transpired.

Now, does this rule mean you should sacrifice your personal integrity or ethics to keep from disagreeing with your boss? Not at all. Never violate your integrity no matter what. What it means is that if you find yourself talking with your boss's boss, make sure your boss knows the content of that conversation as soon as you can.

Respect
This rule reinforces the partnership between you and your boss. It shows your boss you value his perspective and understand his position, and want him to be as completely informed as possible about things going on in the organization. The questions your boss's boss asks will be important to your boss, as will your answers. The fact that you seek out your boss to tell him what happened shows you trust that he won't be angry if you happened to voice an opinion that disagrees with his, especially if he already knows you don't agree and you pointed that out to his boss. Is it a little dicey? Sometimes. Some bosses don't ever

want their people talking to senior management without them. But if you demonstrate that you carry the water when you talk with the big bosses and you accurately and rapidly report conversations and contact to your boss, you'll find yourself on your own with the big bosses more and more. And that means you get to feed bigger bears respect by giving them information—always a tasty morsel.

Results

Do you feed results using this rule? Sure you do. Sometimes your boss wants you to be the one to talk to the big bosses about an issue because you're the expert. And so after your conversation and your opinions are heard, your boss may get a call about the project you're working on and how it needs to be supported more. If your boss has been briefed ahead of time, that call goes a lot smoother, and your boss can then ask for the resources right away because he has the request already in front of him thanks to your quick briefing. And that means results. It also helps you avoid the "come see me" phone call or e-mail when your boss gets blindsided by a "hey, I talked with one of your folks at the picnic and she said…" call from his boss. Avoiding those calls means you have more time to concentrate on what you're doing, which means more results. And more results means less hunger pangs.

RULE TWENTY:

If someone higher in the organization talks to you and makes an inquiry or a casual observation, ensure your boss knows. People in high places and their staffs don't make casual statements.

This one is almost exactly like rule nineteen, with a couple of additions. Members of senior management usually have assistants and staffers who do a lot of question asking and information gathering. Not to mention the questions that senior managers themselves ask. Knowing what they're asking is a valuable piece of information for your boss and for you. If you can anticipate questions, you can head them off by preparing the answers ahead of time in your correspondence or presentations. That means less time working on "we'll get back to you" tasks and more time getting done what you get paid to do.º

Always keep in mind that at work, there really is no small talk. Everything people say and do relates somehow to the job. So keep track of what people ask. Some staffers are big into the margins for error, or the cost/benefit ratio, or the impact on the shareholders. Others always look at how something will impact morale or affect the working environment. These individuals are on the senior management's staff for a reason, and that reason is what you need to understand when dealing with them. For example someone who always wants to see the cost/benefits of programs won't be interested in how the new child-care center will address employee concerns about after-hours child-care availability. But he will be interested in knowing how the onsite child-care center will reduce reimbursable offsite childcare during overtime periods by fifteen percent. Similarly, a staffer who watches morale won't be moved by an argument for removing the televisions in the break room to save money. But she will support removing the televisions and installing a new coffee bar as suggested by recent employee surveys.

Keeping up with who asks what means you know what to say to them when the time comes to get the support you need.

As for casual statements, there aren't any from folks like these. If a higher-up comes into your work area and says, "Wow, the paint in here looks pretty faded," that means you'd better find out when the room was last painted and when you can get it repainted. If you're in charge of the company fleet and one of the senior partners comments at a breakfast meeting that he wonders what the new company cars ride like, you need to let your boss know so together you can arrange a time for that partner to take a ride. Often senior members don't want to come out and say, "You need to paint this room" or, "I want a ride in one of the new cars we're giving out this year" because they don't want to come off as bossy or demanding. So instead they drop hints. When you don't pick up and act upon them, they become orders the next time. And it's much more pleasant for you and your boss if you can see the hint, respond to it, and get the smiles and thanks rather than the, "I want…" phone call.

Respect
Again this rule feeds your immediate boss respect by showing her you acknowledge that she has the experience and perspective to interpret what senior management and their staffers are asking and then design a plan to address it. It shows that you trust your boss with information about what's going on and that your boss is going to use it to help the rest of the organization. And it helps your boss not get blindsided—also a sign of respect.

Results

Can this rule help you get results? Absolutely. By knowing what questions to answer ahead of time, you and your boss will be much better prepared for meetings and conference calls. By anticipating what a staff may ask and preparing an answer tailored to that staffer's area of interest, you eliminate having to answer the question again when they ask it from a more pointed perspective. And being responsive to hints shows that you and your boss are paying attention to the senior members of the organization and creating that "we're all on the same team" feeling among all levels of leadership in the company. These things help you generate results because you're answering questions before they're asked, addressing concerns when they're voiced, and enabling senior leaders to ask for things they want without being demanding. Those results make your boss look good. And bosses who look good rarely come snacking on those who helped them get that way.

RULE TWENTY-ONE:

Paperwork is not the enemy, but it may be your means to defeating the enemy.
What exactly does this mean? Well, it means you should not see paperwork as evil or as a nuisance. It is a tool that, when used properly and in the hands of someone skilled, can get the job done. Defeating the enemy is what military operations are all about, so when I explained to my group of young warriors that now that they were on the staff their main tools for defeating the enemy were briefing papers and memorandums, they looked at me like I was a little off the mark. But it's true. How effective you are at doing paperwork can determine how effective you are at accomplishing whatever your mission happens to be at the time because paperwork does a lot of things for you. It demonstrates the clarity of your ideas. It allows you to package a complete picture of what's happening in a digestible and easily transmitted way. It shows you value the rules and norms of the organization because you complete the paperwork according to the set rules for how paperwork should be done. And it enables you to crystallize the rationale for one proposal versus another in a way that is hard to refute. Let's face it: the words you use have power, and written words have more power than those spoken in a meeting.

Think about it: in our society things that count are almost always written down. Marriage licenses. Deeds to houses. Contracts. Oaths of enlistment. All are written documents usually with signatures at the bottom. Your paperwork has that same power within your organization. It matters. So how it's done matters.

Done properly, your paperwork is an accurate reflection of how hard your folks work each day. Done poorly, it sends a message you don't want: "We don't care enough about what we do to make sure the paperwork is done correctly."

For a lot of your folks, paperwork will be the only way senior members of the organization see what they're doing all day. The reports, memorandums, etc. you produce and submit may be the only chance you get to talk about how great your team is, how hard they work, and how professionally they get the job done. Doesn't the manner in which that message is transmitted need to reflect this? If your paperwork is immaculate and accurate, the impression you create on the reader is the same. And that's why paperwork is important.

Do people dread paperwork? Sure. Most people don't like it at all. And so they fudge it or do just enough to get it through. But there is an advantage to doing paperwork that shines: yours will stand out from the rest, and that may be all it takes to get you and your folks out in front of other sections. And that's how you keep defeating the enemy, whoever it may be: you keep doing what it takes to be chosen. To be out front. To keep winning. Paperwork is the tool for that. It's your report card to your boss on how well things are going. So why wouldn't you make it as top-notch as you can?

Respect
Doing your paperwork well shows you respect the organization, and by respecting the organization you show respect to your boss. You also do this by not wasting your boss's time with paperwork that has to be done over. By giving your boss complete, accurate, and useful products, you arm him with good data that can be used when competing for resources with other divisions, which shows him you respect his ability to do the right thing for you and your folks. Sloppy paperwork sends the message that you don't care and

your boss either doesn't or shouldn't. And that's a huge disrespect sandwich for your bear to chew on. But good, solid paperwork gives your bear a nice snack.

Results

Paperwork typically is either a report on results or the actual result your boss wants. Either way good paperwork is essential to presenting your results accurately. Good paperwork begets more good paperwork, and that means you get more good results. Most of the time poorly done paperwork means you get to do it over. Or your request gets disapproved. Or your proposal gets shot down without consideration. But good paperwork enhances your chances to get more resources and approval for your ideas, and gives you time to get back to work. Those are results hungry bears like to eat.

RULE TWENTY-TWO:

If a suspense lapses and you haven't completed the task, and your boss doesn't ask for the work, don't assume it's been forgotten. The boss won't forget it's due. Neither should you.

A *suspense* is what the military calls a deadline. It's a date and time when something is due. It could be a report, a memorandum, or an answer—pretty much anything that can be expected to be submitted can have a suspense attached to it. There are massive computer programs in use across the world to do nothing more than track suspenses. I know people who put their on-time suspense rate in their performance reports to show how they're getting done what's supposed to be done on time.

So what's this rule about really? It's about your boss trusting you to do what you're supposed to do when you're supposed to do it. And that's it. It's about your boss treating you like a competent professional who can keep track of what's she's tasked you with and then trusting you to do it on time.

Do bosses really keep track of all the things they tell people to do? You bet they do. I know one who has it all written in a little notepad he carries with him. I knew one who kept everything on his computer and updated it faithfully to ensure everything was on track. Trust me, your boss has a system of keeping track of what she's asked for and when it's due. Do not doubt.

So what's the big deal about missing a suspense? Sometimes things happen and you can't get it done in time. Rule twenty-three will address getting extensions and waivers for things, because bosses understand that happens. But if you haven't asked for an extension and you haven't submitted the required product to your boss on time, what message are you sending? You're basically not doing something your boss told you to do. Sure, it's a paperwork exercise, right? I mean, these deadlines aren't that important, are they? Well, they are to your boss, I can assure you. Bosses don't arbitrarily assign deadlines. There's a reason why they need all the reports from all their divisions every Friday afternoon, even if you don't know what the reason is. Maybe they're going to read them on Saturday. Maybe there's a meeting every Monday where all the bosses go over the division status reports from the previous week, and your boss needs hers so she can be ready. Why she needs it by when she needs it is something the boss considers. What you need to do is make sure you can get it to her by that time.

Not meeting the deadline also can send the message that you don't think the deadline or the product is important. It basically sends a message of apathy to your boss—apathy about her authority to impose deadlines and the quality of products you submit. It's a big "who cares?" to your boss. However, she cares or she wouldn't have put a deadline on it in the first place.

Following up on a lapsed deadline isn't the boss's job. Think about it: if she has to track down the week's status report, what does she need you for? She's given you the responsibility, so you need to keep it in mind, watch over it, and make sure it gets done—on time if possible. If it's not on time, don't wait around hoping the boss has forgotten. How would you like it if your boss asked you in a staff meeting for a draft memo that was due two weeks prior? I've seen it happen. It's not pretty.

So you have to stay organized. You have to design a system so you don't miss deadlines. Sometimes people in the military call them suspenses because it's a sport to see what happens to the person who misses the deadline. The suspense of what will happen permeates the office. Don't be that person. Don't be the one to find out what happens.

Respect

Respect for your boss, respect for yourself, respect for the work that's being done. This rule helps transmit all of that. When you meet your suspenses, you're telling your boss you understand her authority to impose deadlines and her ability to prioritize what gets done when, and that you value getting things done when required, just like she does. By ensuring you get your work done on time, you show respect for your responsibilities (given to you by your boss, by the way), respect for the importance of being organized, and that you value getting things done when asked. By completing tasks on time, you show that the work is important. You demonstrate your understanding that it's not busywork but adds value to the organization, and that its being done on time is a mark of professional pride. These respect snacks are tasty treats for your bear, and all it really takes is to keep up with what's due.

Results

This rule is all about results. It's about getting your boss the results she wants on time. By following it you get more latitude to do your job because your boss knows you won't violate the trust she's given you by not getting things done on time. She can give you more leeway in operating because he knows that when the time comes the product will be there. She can also give you the latitude and leeway that enables you to perform, and that means results. It also means your boss has in her possession the products she wants when she wants them, and to her that's results. So feed the bear what she wants.

RULE TWENTY-THREE:

Extensions and waivers can be granted for almost anything, but not if you don't ask. (See rules fifteen and seventeen).

This rule assumes that you understand rule fifteen, about asking your boss so she can say "yes," and rule seventeen, about taking time to do it right the first time. What those rules don't say is that you can get an extension or a waiver just by asking for it. There needs to be a reason; not getting it done on time because you were busy doing something else is not a good reason. Neither is not planning or adequately dividing your time among several priorities. However, there are good reasons sometimes. Conditions change. Priorities change (your boss's, that is). Resources prove inadequate sometimes. There are compelling reasons sometimes to get an extension of a deadline or a waiver of a requirement. But if you don't ask for it, your boss can't grant it.

Is it a little nerve-wracking to ask for an extension? It won't be if you really need it for a good reason. Do you have to phrase it appropriately? Of course. You want to make sure you ask in a way that demonstrates you were putting forth effort and working to meet the deadline, but somehow something changed and now you need more time.

Timing is also crucial for these requests. The time to ask for the extension is as soon as you think you're going to need it. If you wait until the last minute to ask for it, your chances of getting it decrease significantly. But if you ask for the extension as soon as the need arises, you are subtly communicating that you're working on the project, anticipating things that could happen, and taking steps to ensure accomplishment of the mission even if that means moving the deadline. That's proactive. And bosses love to snack on that.

Let's say you have a project due involving the redistribution of existing transportation assets to different divisions inside the organization. And your boss wants the plan by Friday. You have it all ready and you're about to submit it when you learn that the leases on the vehicles you've been using won't be renewed. And it's Thursday. Do you ask for the extension? Of course you do. Your plan won't work as it is, and you don't want to give your boss a worthless product just to meet a deadline. So you go and explain that you have a plan based on what you knew on Wednesday, but now you've just learned that the conditions have changed. Does your boss want to see the old plan (in case she wants to fight to get the leases renewed and then use your old plan) or does she want to give you a few days to develop a new plan based on the new information? Now the decision is up to her. You've demonstrated initiative, you've anticipated her questions (Why do you need an extension? Do you have the old plan? Etc.), and you're prepared to give her what you've already accomplished. What will most bosses say in this situation? "Let me have what you put together already, then go back and work up a new plan without the current lease and let me see it by Wednesday." Have you saved yourself work? Maybe. Did you feed your bear good stuff? Certainly.

Respect
Does your boss feel respected when you ask for an extension? Sure. It shows her that you know she's in charge and has the ability to grant requests. Does it demonstrate your commitment to meeting suspenses and getting things done right the first time? It does in a big way. Especially if you keep your boss up to speed on how things are going with important projects and steps along the way where

she can help. Sometimes you get an extension without even asking for it. If you let your boss know how it's going along the way, she may ask if you need more time to make sure it's done right. If you think you need it, take it. But don't take advantage of it. Meeting deadlines is a sign you can perform what needs to be done when it needs to be done. Asking for extensions means you understand that doing it on time is important, but doing it right is critical. And bosses like to feel like they're the ones who determine what's important and what's critical (they prioritize, remember). Granting extensions is their way of showing you what's critical. And that's you feeding them respect.

Results

Do you get results you can feed your bear? You do if you get the extension. You get results that are usable and useful for your boss, and bosses want usable and useful. Just meeting the deadline isn't what she wants. The deadline isn't arbitrary, nor should your asking for an extension be. The extension should be to ensure you can meet the deadline not just to the letter of the requirement but also in spirit. Making sure you give the boss not only what she asked for but what she meant when she asked for it is a huge part of your job. And the extension may be what you need to do that. So it generates results you can use—the tasty kind your boss craves.

RULE TWENTY-FOUR:

Keep track of who you've talked to and when.

Does this seem like something you need to do to take care of your boss? Sure it does. Keeping track of who you spoke to and when you spoke to them makes it so much easier when disagreements and misunderstandings arise. I mean, there are never any rumors where you work, are there? No one ever says one thing in one meeting to one set of people and then something different on the same topic in another meeting do they? These things don't happen, right?

If you keep track of who you speak to and when, I can guarantee this won't happen to you very often. Once people realize you not only listen to what they say but can repeat when and where they said it, they'll ensure what they say to you is what they say to anyone and everyone. And that makes it easier on your boss.

No one likes rumors. No one likes gossip. Keeping track of who said what makes it so you and your boss are operating on facts, not gossip. You're operating with hard data, and that's tough to argue with.

So how do you do this? If you're using e-mail, read receipts are critical. And sent items files. You need to keep them. They not only show what you did and when you did it, but they record that the other person received it. For phone calls and face-to-face meetings, the best sources for recording who said what and when are memorandums for record, signed by you. I have saved a lot of time and effort over the years by using these techniques. They make it easier when someone comes back and says, "But you said...." Then you can bring out a memorandum documenting the date, time, and place of the meeting and what was actually said by certain people. Once word gets out—and it will—that you have that kind of documentation, people will be very reluctant to try to say you said something when you didn't. Or they won't try to say one thing to you at one point and another thing at another point. They'll realize you're actually listening, and that will mean people won't say things in your meetings just to say them. They'll understand you'll hold them to whatever they promise in public, so they have to make sure they can back it up when the time comes.

The main thing this rule helps reduce is the "they say" syndrome. You know about this—it's what happens when people get together at work and begin to talk about things. Sooner or later the rumors about promotions, transfers, etc. start, and sooner or later someone says, "They say...." And pretty soon whatever "they" said gets around, and people start to believe it even though usually there is no basis for it. Unchecked, the smoke and shadow become reality.

You can reduce what "they" say by making sure you can credit who told you what and when. Then when you speak, it's with authority, and rumors are reduced. Reduced rumors mean you or your boss spend less time tracking them down. And that means more time for actual, meaningful work.

Respect
This rule enables you to inform you boss with facts. It does not ask your boss to make assumptions about where you got your information or how you know what you know. This rule helps you keep track of what is actually taking place and credit your sources, and that shows respect. It's like when you write a paper for college or high school and you have to cite your sources. The same principle applies. The rest of whatever you write has more weight because

you're not afraid to say where you got the information. That shows respect to your boss. It's letting him decide for himself how credible the information is based on where it came from and what that means. Letting the boss decide is always a good thing and always reduces the hunger pangs.

Results

Do you get results with this rule? To be certain. People will know they need to be completely honest when dealing with you because you are paying attention. And people like it when others pay attention. The next part is that you hold people accountable for what they say, and that will make them more inclined to do what they say and say what they do. That produces results. It also reduces the rumor mill, and that helps you concentrate on actual work, which is what produces results. And results are what keep your boss well fed.

RULE TWENTY-FIVE:

Writing things down develops and enforces discipline of thought. If you can't put it on paper, keep thinking.

Why is this a rule? Writing was something you had to do in high school, so why is it so important to your boss? Because words have power. And written words have even more. So the simple act of writing it down is not something that can be done lightly or without thought. Especially if your name is going to be attached to it. Why would your boss want you to write things down? So you think them through. Pie-in-the-sky thinking doesn't give you actionable plans.

Does this mean there's no place for brainstorming or time spent in thought? Of course not. What it means is that the brainstorming or thinking is without value unless you put it on paper. Unless the thinking leads to doing, it's really daydreaming, and that's not what your boss pays you to do. The bridge between an idea and an action will likely be a piece of paper with words on it. Your boss wants your ideas, but he wants your ideas to be useful and usable. So you need to write them down somewhere.

You will have great ideas if you pay attention, but those great ideas will do no one any good if they don't become some kind of action or project or program. So you need to figure out a way to capture your ideas and put them on paper. And as "wouldn't it be great if…" kinds of things—put some meat on them. Flesh out why they're great ideas. Talk about how they would benefit the organization or how they would make existing processes better, or anything that links the ideas to something of value. Then talk about how the ideas can be made into realities. You don't have to have all the answers, but at least keep thinking through what it would take.

Keep your ideas somewhere you can access them, and look over them from time to time. Once in a while, you'll see an opportunity in a staff meeting or a conference to voice your ideas. If you've already got most of them on paper in forms that make sense, you can even slip them to your boss as proposals, and they may take on lives of their own.
Take the time to think through your ideas and put them on paper so one day they'll be more than just ideas.

Respect

You feed your boss respect with this rule by giving him a clear message that you respect his time and interests. You convey this message by paying attention to what's happening around you and thinking of ways to make it better, and doing so in a systematic, organized way. In addition you write it down so it's not lost. You take time to create frameworks for the future in the form of your ideas put to paper. This shows you respect the organization and want to see it succeed, and that makes your boss feel respected as well. And you're not just making things up without having thought about it, wasting everyone's time on things that sound good but aren't possible because of X, Y and Z. By thinking through it, you've overcome those limitations and are showing how it can be done, saving a lot of people—most notably your boss—from wasting a lot of time on figuring out how your great idea could be made into reality. And bears live in reality, so the more things you can do to make reality better, the less hungry they get.

Results

This rule focuses on results down the line more than those immediately available or visible. But it eventually gets you to where you're feeding results to the boss because you're using what you know and putting it with what you think in a format that can be used to make things better. The better things are, the less hungry your bear becomes.

RULE TWENTY-SIX:

Bosses speak with a purpose. If they make a suggestion, it's an order. Using "please" and "could you" is really just them being polite. Make no mistake: they're not talking to hear themselves talk.

Most people don't stop to think what their bosses do all day. In fact until you get to be a boss, you don't give it much thought. What most leaders and managers in organizations do all day is talk: to subordinates, to peers, to customers, to their bosses.... They talk a lot. In fact I usually spend so much time at work talking, when I get home I don't want to talk at all to anyone. At least not for a while.

So when your boss does come and say something to you, regardless of when or where it is, there's a reason for it. Bosses generally like it quiet, and they generally don't have as much time to sit quietly and think and plan as they would like, so they're not going to waste time and effort on saying something just to say something. They expect to say it one time and that's it. You really want to get your bear riled up? Make him tell you to do something more than once. The first time it may sound like it's a favor or a "nice to do" kind of thing. It's not. He expects you to do it because he took the time to say it. So if you don't, the second time it may not be so pleasant. And by the third time he's had to tell you to do something, you might as well get out the honey, because it's going to be a one-sided conversation.

So what do you need to do? You need to pay attention. You need to learn how your boss chooses to communicate. Some bosses are very direct and self-aware, and they'll tell you how they're going to communicate with you. These bears are the easiest when it comes to knowing what they want from what they say. They'll tell you that they ask for things specifically in e-mails or by memorandums and if it's not written down, they aren't really asking. Others may say if you hear the words "I would like…" they expect you to take it as an instruction or order. If your bear is aware of how he communicates, your life is easier and harder—easier because you know what to look for, harder because there's no excuse for missing what he wants due to miscommunication.

But what if your bear isn't aware of how he communicates? That means you need to be paying attention. Or you need to ask him. This is an especially good technique when you first get assigned to a new boss. Usually you'll get some time to ask questions about how he likes to do things, and some good ones are: How do you like to communicate? Do you like e-mail? Do you prefer one-on-one meetings with your managers? Do you make food-for-thought comments or are your suggestions the things you want to see happen? If your boss opens the dialogue about how he operates, get in there and ask.

Now, what happens if your boss tells you he doesn't think everything she suggests is an order, but in fact it is? Well, you figured it out, right? So just operate according to the rule. You won't go wrong assuming that every request or suggestion from your boss is an order. But not doing so could be disastrous.

Respect
This is a big respect nugget, especially for bosses who like to think of themselves as low-maintenance when in fact they are high-maintenance. If you can listen to what your boss says and glean from it the things he wants done and then do them, you're feeding him respect. You're anticipating what he wants, you're listening to what he says, and

then you're out there doing what he wants done, and that's really what most bosses want. And you're doing it in a way that doesn't force him to say, "Do this, this, and this, and that's an order." There aren't many bosses who like to say, "That's an order." Even in the military it's not done, especially not like in the movies and on television. Why? Because of respect. If the senior person says "do it," it's an order. He doesn't have to include the words "this is an order" to make it one. The respect for the authority of the person issuing the instruction makes it an order. The same thing applies to your boss. Making him say it's a directive or an order undermines his authority. Your doing it because he suggested it reinforces his authority, and that's a huge respect treat to feed your bear.

Results

Does your boss get results with this rule? To be sure. Especially when you're paying attention and anticipating based on what he suggests. Your boss will get the results he asks for without having to formally ask, and that's a big treat for him. And it's good for you because you get to spend time working on things that will pay dividends for you and your folks, and you will do so knowing it's what the boss wants, which makes for better and more-effective results. Bosses love to eat more-effective results whenever they can.

RULE TWENTY-SEVEN:

When you speak, do so with precision.

What does this mean? And why does your boss want you to speak a certain way? It has nothing to do with whether you speak with an accent or if you speak quickly or slowly. The focus of this rule is precision. Words have power whether you realize it or not and whether you use them or not. The words you use are important, and your boss knows this. That's why your need to speak with precision and understand how your words will impact your audience. You need to ensure, like your mother told you, that if you don't have something good to say, you don't say anything at all. Now, she was talking about being nice to people and that kind of thing. And that's important. But there is also *good* in the sense of choosing the proper word at the proper time, and not using hot-button words that set people off and turn a meeting from a discussion into a riot.

Think about it: You know some words will automatically set people off. And they should. There are words in our society that are so heavily laden with history and meaning that to speak them is to invite controversy or contention. So you need to ensure you do not use them. You want people to listen to your message, not be caught up on onc or two words that are such distracters they become detractors.

So what do you do? You find the words that distract people in your organization and choose not to use them. Or do so, if you're trying to distract people. Sometimes you will want to, but not as a matter of regular operations.

What are those words? You have to pay attention to discover that. And once you do, make sure you pass that knowledge on to your peers and your subordinates. You don't want to have to explain why your best team leader was heard using the boss's most hated slang term in the boss's presence. If that happens you'll be feeding part of yourself to your bear, I can assure you.

Now, some people will say the message is the important part, or the words aren't important as long as you don't use profanity or insults or slurs. But let me give you an example. On most military bases, there are *host* units that are responsible for the infrastructure and the majority of what happens on the bases. These units control when the gates open, when the dining facilities will serve meals, when the fitness centers will be open, and hundreds of other things that make military bases run. On most bases there are also what are commonly called *tenant* units. These units have a specific mission and are located on the same base as the host, but they don't control a lot of the resources or services their folks need and use. And so for years, hosts called the tenants just that: tenants. And even though a tenant unit may have a commander of equal or even greater rank than the host's, the host has huge amounts of control. So in public forums, on web sites, and in written welcome letters and packages, the term tenant has been used. How do you think that has made the members of those units feel? Do you think they feel welcomed on the bases where they live and work? Do you think they really feel like they're part of what goes on at the installation? Probably not. Why? Because *tenant* is a word that implies a lack of power and authority, and subordinate priority when compared to the host.

On one base I was on, the host unit got a new commander, and at one of his first staff meetings someone referred to the tenant units. The commander stopped the meeting and looked all his subordinate unit commanders in the eyes as he said, "There are no *tenants* on this base. We have *partners* here. Their mission is equally critical to the defense of our nation, and they are in no way less than our complete equals. They are our partners and will be referred to as such. I don't want to hear them called tenants again by anyone in any forum."

How do you think that made people feel? How do you think that changed the dynamics among the units on the installation? If you don't think changing that one term made a difference, you are very, very mistaken. The words you use have power. Speaking precisely enables you to use that power in a way that helps you, your boss, and the organization. And your boss wants you to use it.

Respect

Speaking precisely shows respect for your boss because it means you value her time and aren't going to waste it with a lot of "ums" and "uhs" and "you knows" that have no value. It shows that you understand communication is a critical component to continued success and the words you use are important. It means you've thought through what you're attempting to communicate to the point where you can articulate it without pregnant pauses, slang, jargon, spontaneous utterances, or verbal miscues. It feeds your boss respect because you're getting straight to the point with words that are exactly what should be said. You're respecting the boss by not asking her to translate your rambling, verbose soliloquy into a coherent, concise thought on the subject. And respecting the bear means the bear will be less likely to snack on you.

Results

Do you get results when you speak with precision? You bet you do. When you choose your words carefully and ensure they are the correct ones, you eliminate much confusion, ambiguity, and misunderstanding. And those things can cause delays, misplaced priorities, or even people flat-out doing the wrong thing. When you avoid using hot-button words that get people riled, you don't have to schedule meetings to handle the fallout. Speaking precisely enables you to keep things professional and prevents personality conflicts from taking over or even entering the equation, and that enables you to stay focused on the task at hand, which means results. It reduces distractions, and less distractions means more action. More action means more results. And more results means a much less hungry bear.

RULE TWENTY-EIGHT:

When you write, do it right.

Sounds a lot like rule twenty-seven, doesn't it? That's because if you can speak precisely, you need to be able to write that way as well. You know that somewhere in your organization, someone does nothing but sit around with the Harbrace College Handbook and Strunk and White's *The Elements of Style* and try to find the grammatical or stylistic errors in people's memorandums, presentations, and staff packages. And that person is probably in a position to whisper continually to the boss about who writes well and who doesn't. Now, is your writing correct? Probably. There's no rule, really, about ending sentences with *ly* except that some people think it's not correct. So you need to figure out what book he uses and make sure what you write is what he expects. Why go to all this trouble, especially if he may or may not be correct? Because he has the positional power and he thinks he's correct. And he sits next to the boss. Why does your boss care? Because you may be right, and if you push it you'll put her in the awkward position of having to choose between you and her assistant. That's not fun, especially when it can be avoided.

So figure out what it takes to get your correspondence through the first time. Remember: the main goal is to get the memo or the proposal signed or approved. If that means you use the Oxford comma then that's what you do. Or don't do, as the case may be.

The second main reason why this is an important rule is because words, as we have seen, have power. And written words have even more impact. So if you write it right, it gets more notice and generates even more power as it moves up the chain. So if there's a typographical error or a huge mistake in grammar or diction, sooner or later someone will notice, and that may be all it takes to derail the plan. So learn when to use *ensure* instead of *insure* or *principal* instead of *principle*, and especially *affect* versus *effect*. These are commonly misused words that someone who knows the difference will recognize and could potentially use to call into question the validity of your entire argument. Don't give them that chance.

Respect
This rule respects your boss by making it easier on her, especially by not making her choose between you and whoever reviews her correspondence. Keeping the interoffice conflicts to a minimum is always a good thing, and this rule helps you do that for your boss by not picking a grammar fight with her language czar. It also respects your boss by giving her something that's written so it doesn't require tweaking or editing before passing it forward. It is written so the words speak for themselves and are easy to pass up the chain without modification, giving your boss back some time she can use to work on other things. And that's always a great thing to feed your bear.

Results
Do you get results with this rule? If you follow it you do. Because it will mean less time spent arguing with people about what rule you both learned in high school English class applies, which will give you back time to work on your real job. The cleaner and more precise your written correspondence is, the easier a time you will have getting it through the wickets and approved or signed. And that means, depending on what kind of written product it is, you may get your additional resources more quickly, your new hires onboard in a shorter time, or your new project approved this week rather than next. That means more time to work on results. And results are always tasty.

RULE TWENTY-NINE:

Lastly, only you know if you gave one hundred percent to everything you did that day. Your boss can gauge and get close, but only you will truly know if you gave it all you had. Your one hundred percent is all that can be expected. It's also all that should be accepted. If you think doing the minimum is good enough, let your boss know. You can be sure they'll help you find somewhere else to spend your time, because you're wasting theirs.

Sounds kind of harsh, right? Maybe. But if you're miserable and you hate your job, you're not going to be giving it your one hundred percent. Now, this amount will likely vary from day to day, because things outside of work do affect you. But if you're working as hard as you can each day, your boss will be able to tell, and you'll be able to tell as well. You owe it to yourself to give the maximum effort you can each day. It's a matter of personal integrity. Your name is on some piece of your organization's product each day. That should matter to you. If it doesn't you need to look for something else to do. You spend the majority of your time each week at work. And more and more people are spending more and more time at work. If you're not going to give your best effort to the place you give most of your time to, you're cheating not only the organization but yourself as well.

Your boss wants your best effort. Bosses are pretty good at evaluating whether or not you're putting it all on the line on a daily basis.

If you're not, they'll know. And eventually they'll take steps to let you do what you do somewhere else. Don't let that happen. If you want to work there, give your one hundred percent. If you don't, find somewhere else. And be honest with your boss about it. Let him help you. Go to him and let him know you're not the right fit (it happens a lot) and see if he'll be willing to help you find somewhere that is. He will, I'm sure. Why? Because he wants someone who is the right fit, just like you want to be somewhere that is the right fit. Being honest with each other will help you both find the right person for the right place, even if it's not with each other.

Respect
This is a huge respect nugget for your boss. If you're giving one hundred percent, it shows you value the organization, its rules, its principles, and especially your boss's leadership. It demonstrates you want to be there and want to do well, and that feeds your boss lots of respect. If you don't want to be there and you're open and honest about it, that shows your boss respect as well, enough not to waste his time or money by staying when you'd rather be elsewhere. It means you value his time just as he does, and you won't waste it by being a drain on his resources when you'd rather be somewhere else doing something else. So give your best to your boss and she'll do his best to take care of you. That's a good recipe for both of you.

Results
If you're giving one hundred percent, you'll get results. If you're paying attention to the things you've read so far, you'll be feeding your boss respect and results on a consistent basis, and your maximum effort will only increase the quality and quantity of results you feed your boss. Being honest about not wanting to be there also feeds your boss results because a boss would rather have a good employee who gives one hundred percent each day than a supremely gifted employee who only does the minimum. So give it your best or give it a rest. Just make sure you're open and honest with your boss about it and you'll feed him good results, which is what a boss really wants.

Dessert

Something to Chew On

So there it is, at least for now: twenty-nine rules about how to take care of your boss. Now, notice all these rules are about taking care of your boss, which is only a small part of your job. You still have to do whatever it is you get paid you get paid for, or else you won't have any results of any kind. But these rules will help you as you interact with your boss and will give you back time so you can work on whatever it is you do, whether it's running a section, programming a system, supervising line employees, or maybe turning wrenches on a line. Whatever you do, these rules will help you interact with the person who pays you for doing it so you won't be in your bear's lair for not getting the job done. That's no fun.

What to do now? Take these rules and see how many will work where you work. The ones that require a little research (priorities, pet peeves, hot-button words, etc,) will take you a while to investigate before you're ready to implement. Others you can apply right away (keeping track of who you talk to, not putting people on hold, etc.). The main thing is not to be afraid to talk openly and honestly with your boss about how you can best meet her expectations. Don't be afraid to ask about how she wants you to communicate or how she wants you

Something to Chew On

to interpret casual comments. If you don't ask or talk to her, she can't explain it to you. And it's much easier to have that conversation before rather than after.

What happens if you don't do anything with these rules? Maybe nothing. But then again your boss has a boss. And your boss may think of her boss as a bear, just like you think of your boss as one. Which means she may be reading this book as well. Who knows, your boss may even have given you a copy of this book. Which means she knows what the book says. So if she knows you should be doing these things and you aren't…might as well get out the honey.

After-Dinner Mint

About the Author

Dr. Kenneth Woodcock began studying leadership at a very early age and hopes to continue to learn more with each passing year. After graduating from high school, he enrolled at Duke University, where he studied Economics and Russian Language and Literature.

About the Author

Upon graduating, he entered the United States Air Force. Along the way, he attending the University of North Carolina at Chapel Hill, where he graduated with a Master of Public Administration degree. However, since his mother always wanted him to be a doctor, he continued his education and received his Doctor of Management from Webster University. A veteran of two tours of duty in Iraq, he was also a Presidential Management Fellow in Washington, D.C. and currently serves as a member of the Air Force Reserve. In addition to his civilian education, he graduated from the Air Force's Air Command and Staff College and Air War College. He and his wife (who is amazing and far more talented than he) make their home together wherever the Air Force sees fit to send them.

Take Out Menu

A Quick Reference After the Meal

Now that you've gotten to this point, you may want to have a page you can turn to and refresh your memory on all the rules. You may also want to, at some point, come back and look up a rule or two. This reference will enable you to do so by listing the rules and the page in the book where you can find it. Enjoy!

1. Never, never do or allow anything illegal, unethical, immoral, or stupid. [9]

2. Know your boss's priorities. Work those as if they were your own because if you don't prioritize like your boss, your boss will reprioritize for you. Know your boss's boss's priorities too, and how what you're doing fits. If you don't know the priorities, ask. [13]

3. Don't hesitate to ask your boss what to do if you're uncertain about anything. [17]

A Quick Reference After the Meal

4. Don't ever sign your boss's name to anything. [19]

5. Avoid "The Boss Wants" syndrome. [21]

6. Never keep anyone waiting on the phone. Call back. [23]

7. If you say you're going to get back to someone, ensure you do, and do it in a timely manner. [27]

8. Be available to anyone who wants to see you. Never treat people like you're busy or too important to listen to what they have to say. [29]

9. If it's an emergency, you'll know. If it isn't, take time to analyze and think before you act, speak, or write. Get someone to read over your e-mail, paper, or staff package before you hit "send." [33]

10. No surprises. Bad news doesn't get better with time. [37]

11. If there is a problem brewing, your boss will want to know about it early, so give them a heads-up as soon as possible. Bosses don't like being blindsided. [41]

12. There's no such thing as too much relevant information on an issue. Stick to the facts and leave your ego and emotion at home. [45]

13. Punctuality is the courtesy of kings. Be punctual; don't waste anyone's time, especially your boss's or your own. [49]

14. Meetings should be uninterrupted and an interactive exchange. Ask a lot of questions. Discussion and debate are part of the development process. Once the boss decides, though, debate ends and you move out. [53]

15. If you don't ask, your boss can't say "yes." [57]

16. No one knows your job better than you do. After all, you're the one doing it. So no one is in a better position to make suggestions for improvements than you are. If you have an idea for how to make something better and you don't voice it, you can't blame anyone but yourself if things don't change for the better. See rules 10 and 15. [59]

17. Take the time to do it right because there is not always time to do it over. And doing it over usually requires an explanation of why it wasn't done right in the first place. [63]

18. Be your boss's best source of information on what's happening. [65]

19. If you've briefed your boss's boss on something, ensure you brief your boss on it too. [69]

20. If someone higher in the organization talks to you and makes an inquiry or an observation, ensure your boss knows. People in high places and their staffs don't make casual statements. [73]

21. Paperwork is not the enemy, but it may be your means to defeating the enemy. [77]

22. If a suspense lapses and you haven't completed the task, and your boss doesn't ask for the work, don't assume it's been forgotten. The boss won't forget it's due. Neither should you. [81]

23. Extensions and waivers can be granted for almost anything, but not if you don't ask. (See rules 15 and 17). [85]

24. Keep track of who you've talked to and when. [89]

25. Writing things down develops and enforces discipline of thought. If you can't put it on paper, keep thinking. [93]

A Quick Reference After the Meal

26. Bosses speak with a purpose. If they make a suggestion, it's an order. Using "please" and "could you" is really just them being polite. Make no mistake: they're not talking to hear themselves talk. [95]

27. When you speak, do so with precision. [99]

28. When you write, do it right. [103]

29. Lastly, only you know if you gave one hundred percent to everything you did that day. The boss can gauge and get close, but only you will truly know if you gave it all you had. Your one hundred percent is all that can be expected. It's also all that should be accepted. If you think doing the minimum is good enough, let your boss know. You can be sure they'll help you find somewhere else to spend your time, because you're wasting theirs. [105]

Made in the USA
Middletown, DE
14 April 2025